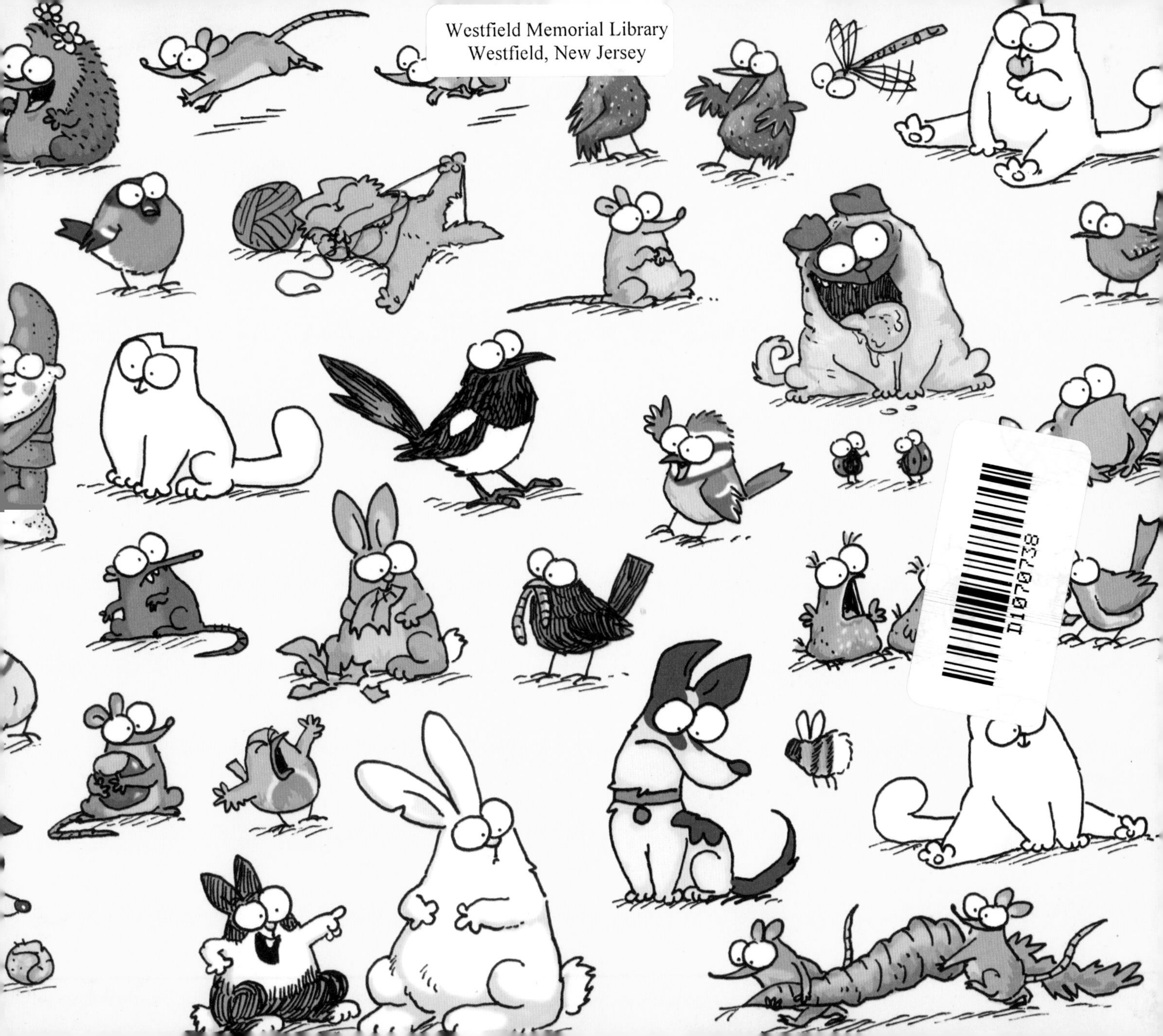

Simon's Cat ®

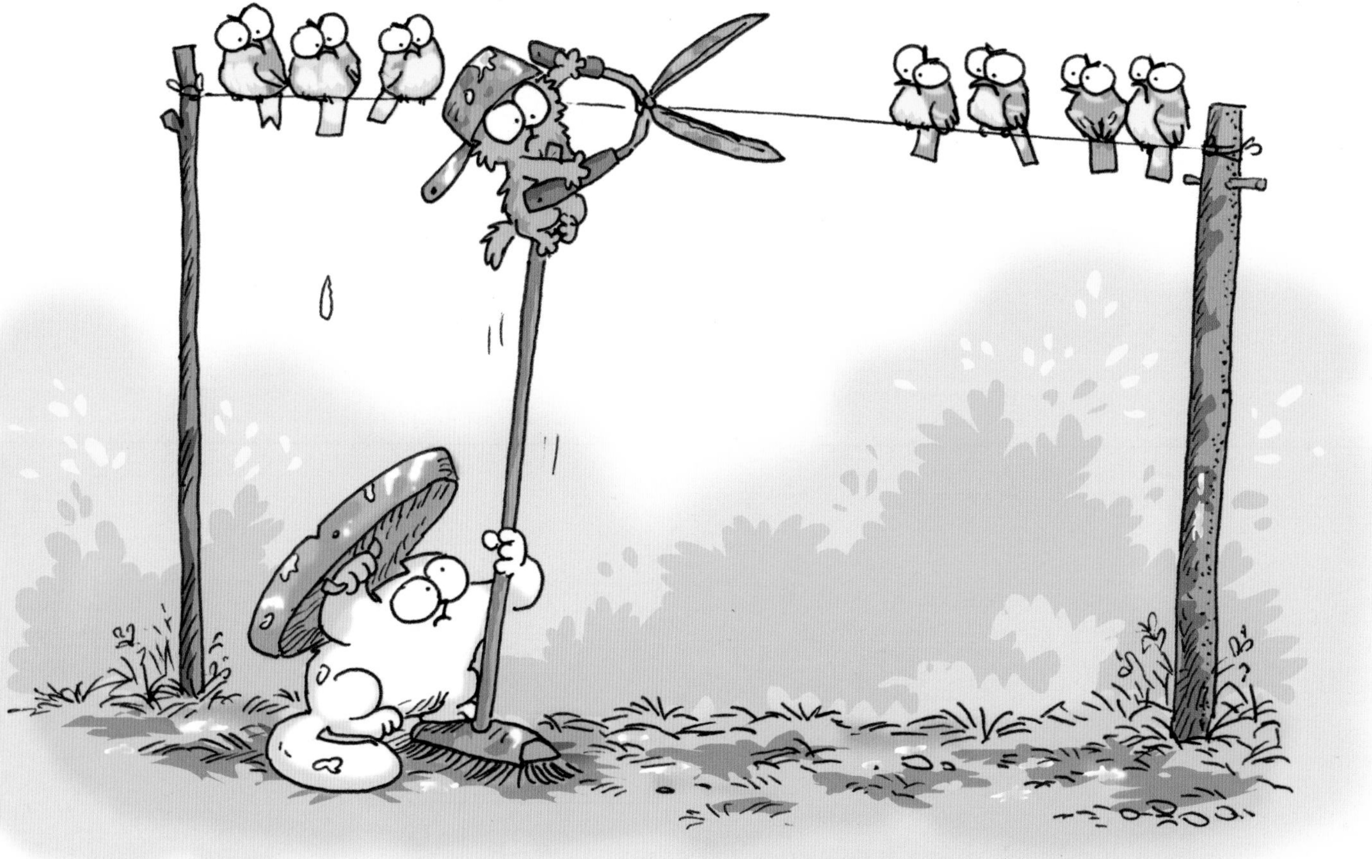

Simon's Cat® vs. THE WORLD

Simon Tofield

AKASHIC BOOKS

Published in the United States by Akashic Books
Published by arrangement with Canongate Books Ltd, 14 High Street, Edinburgh EH1 1TE
©2012, 2013 Simon Tofield

ISBN-13: 978-1-61775-188-2
Library of Congress Control Number: 2013937569
Typeset by Simon's Cat

First Akashic Books printing

Akashic Books
PO Box 1456
New York, NY 10009
info@akashicbooks.com
www.akashicbooks.com

Printed in China

For my Zoë

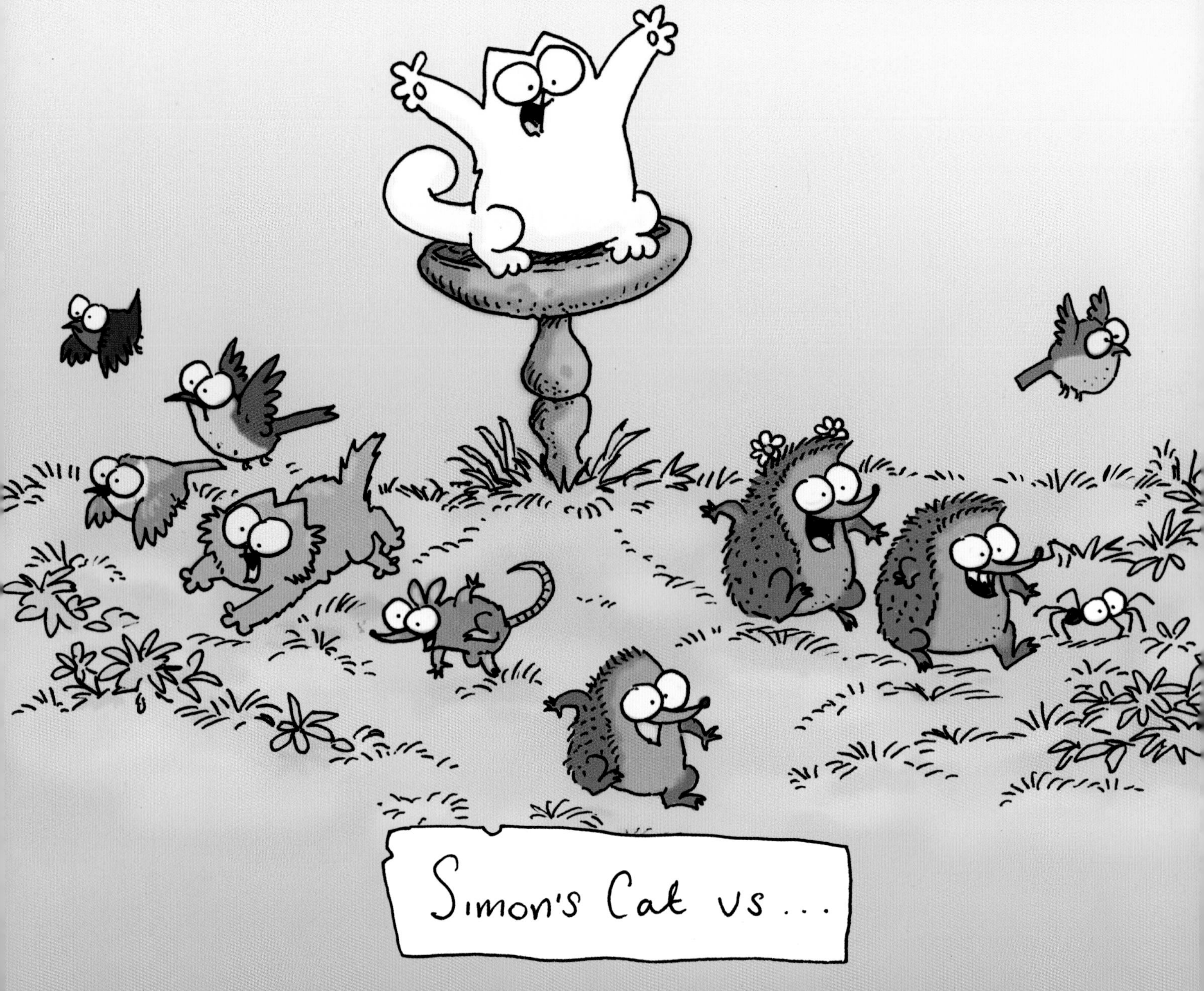
Simon's Cat vs . . .

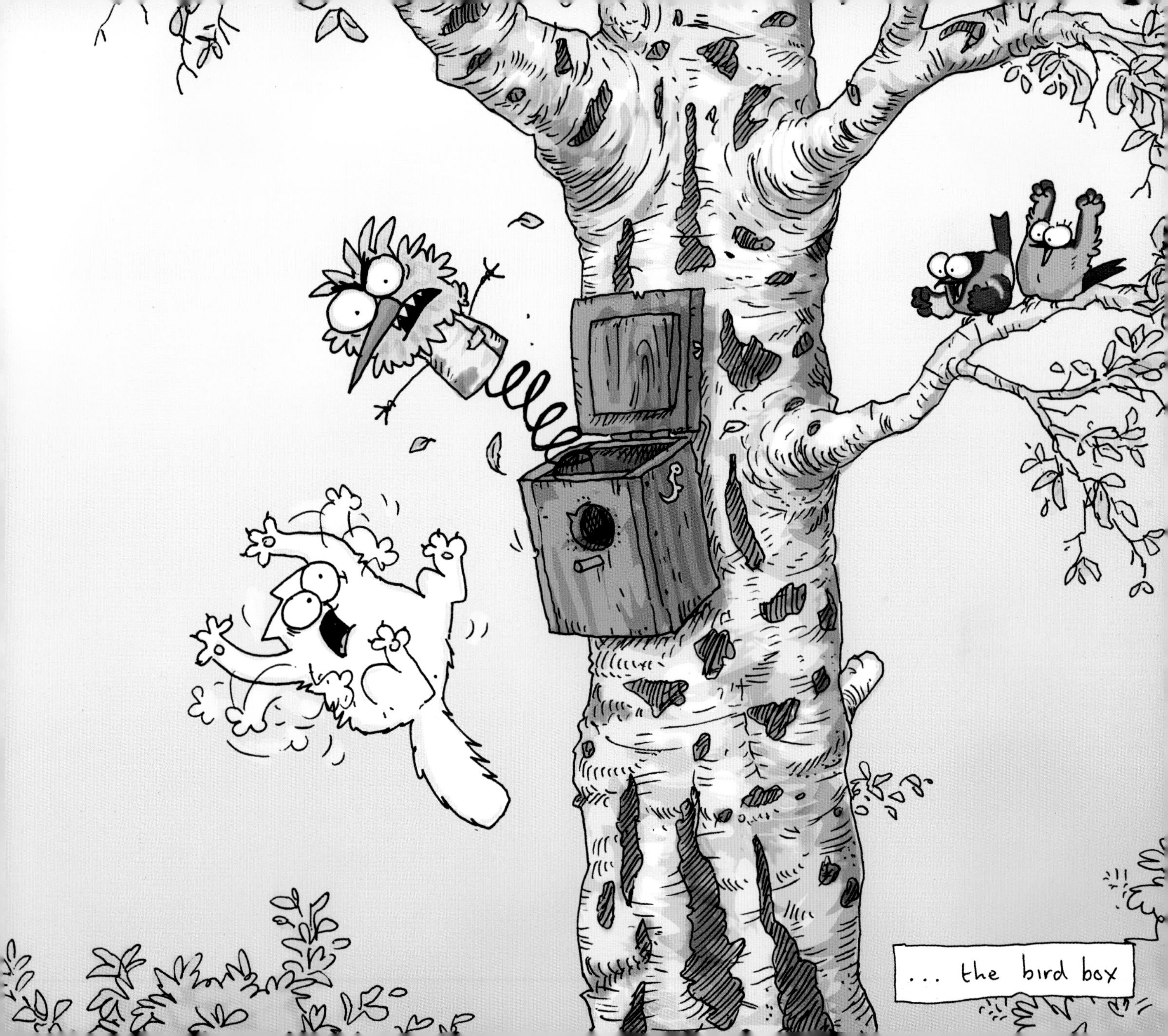
... the bird box

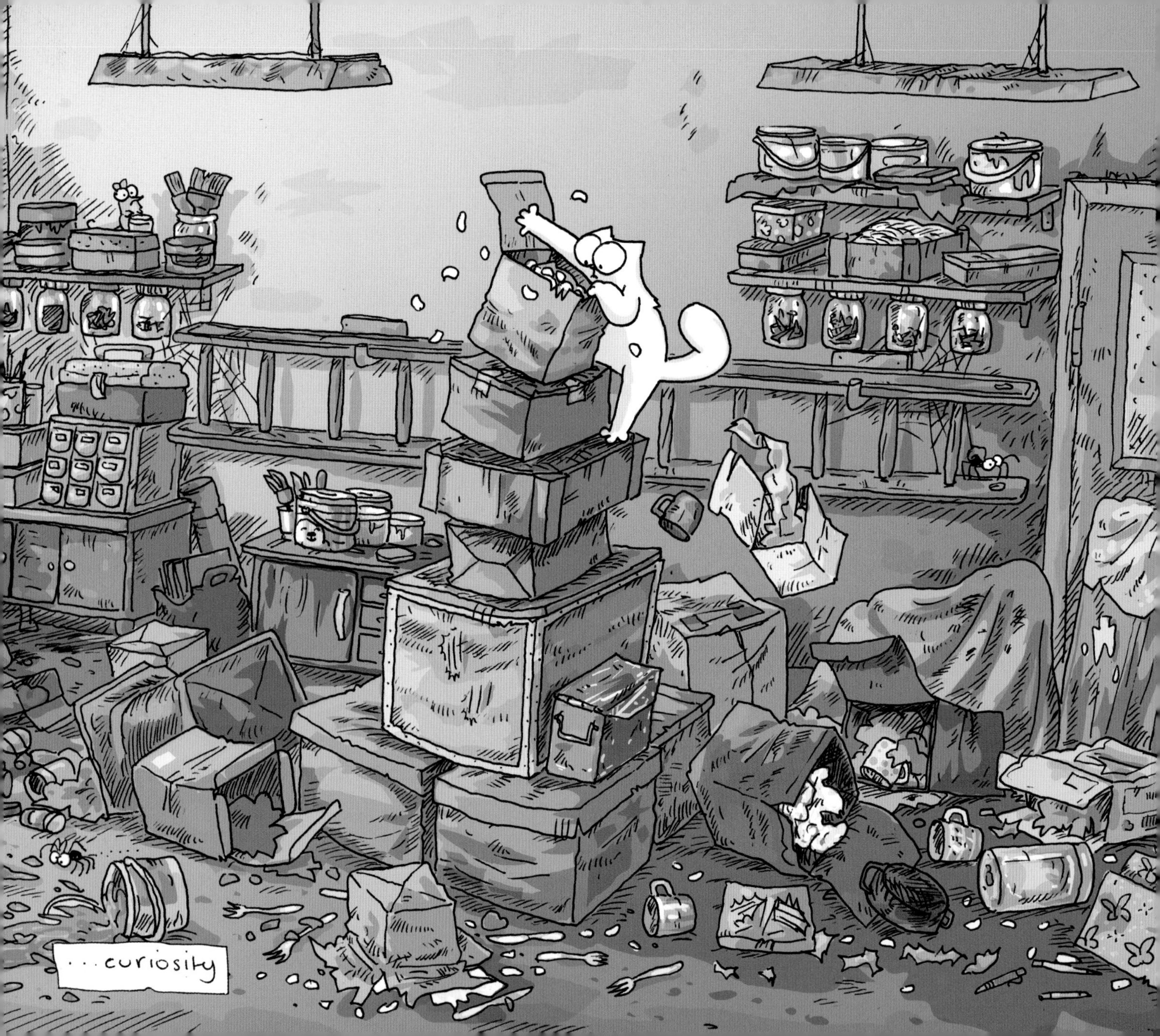
. . . curiosity

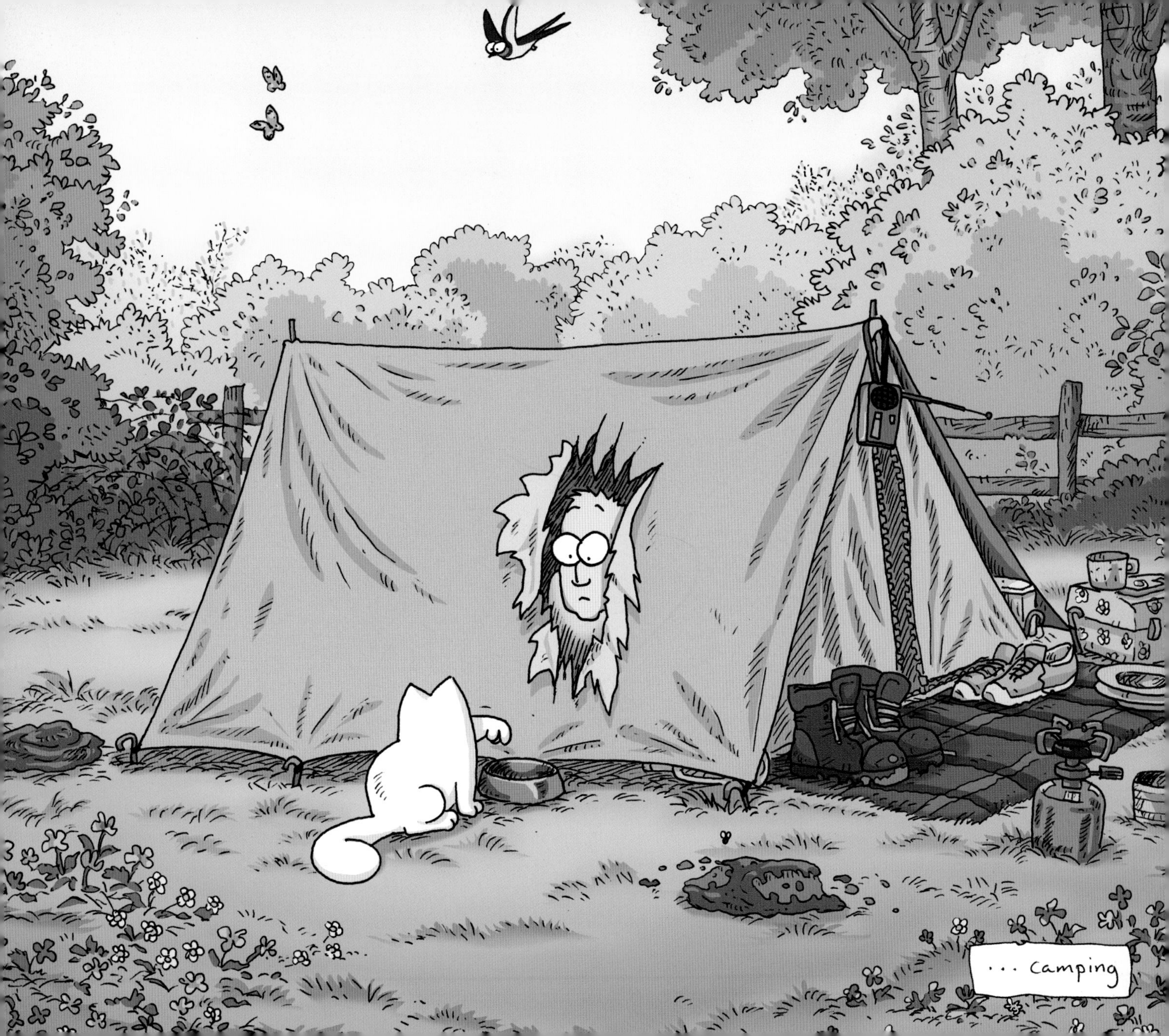
. . . Camping

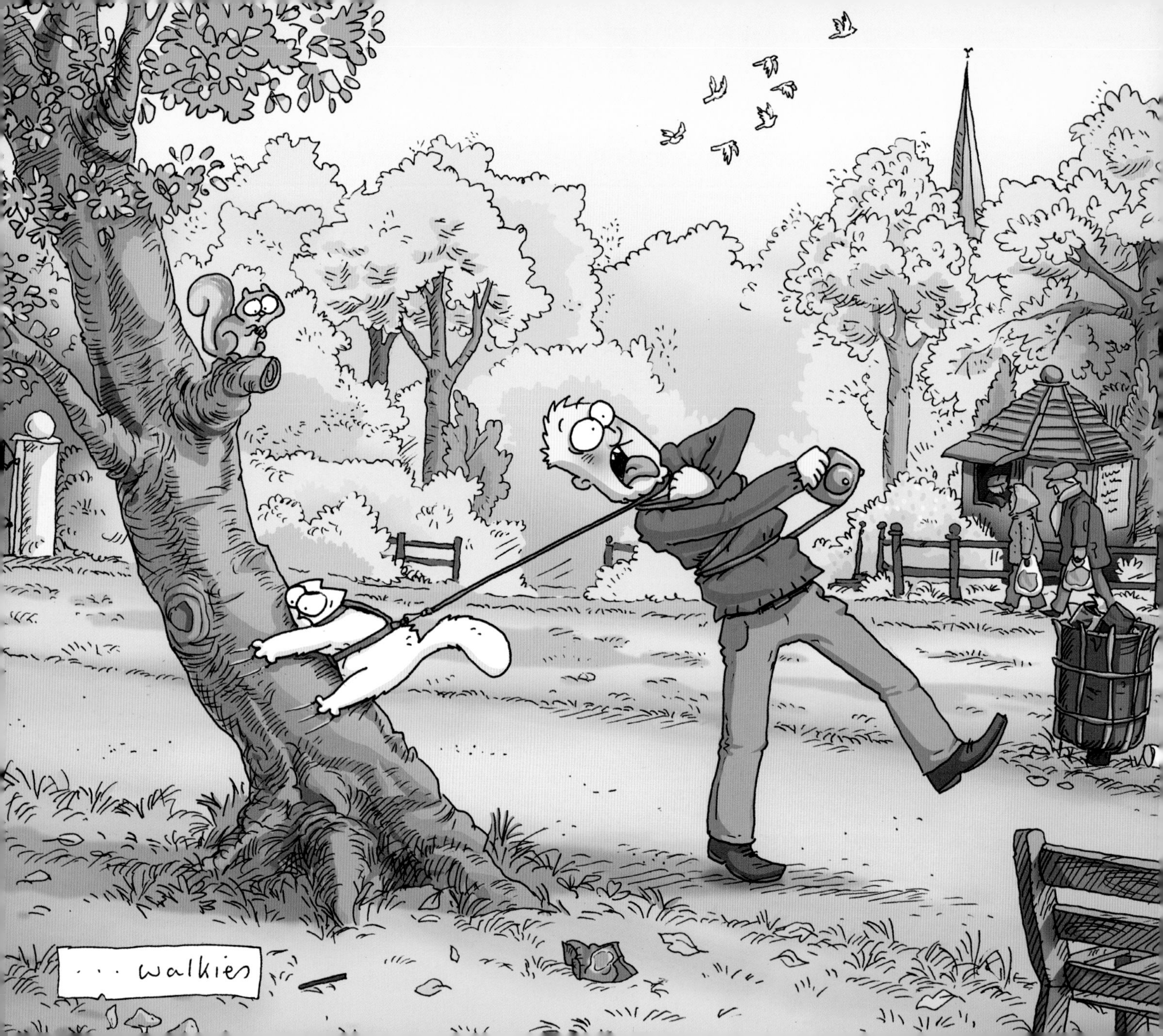
. . . walkies

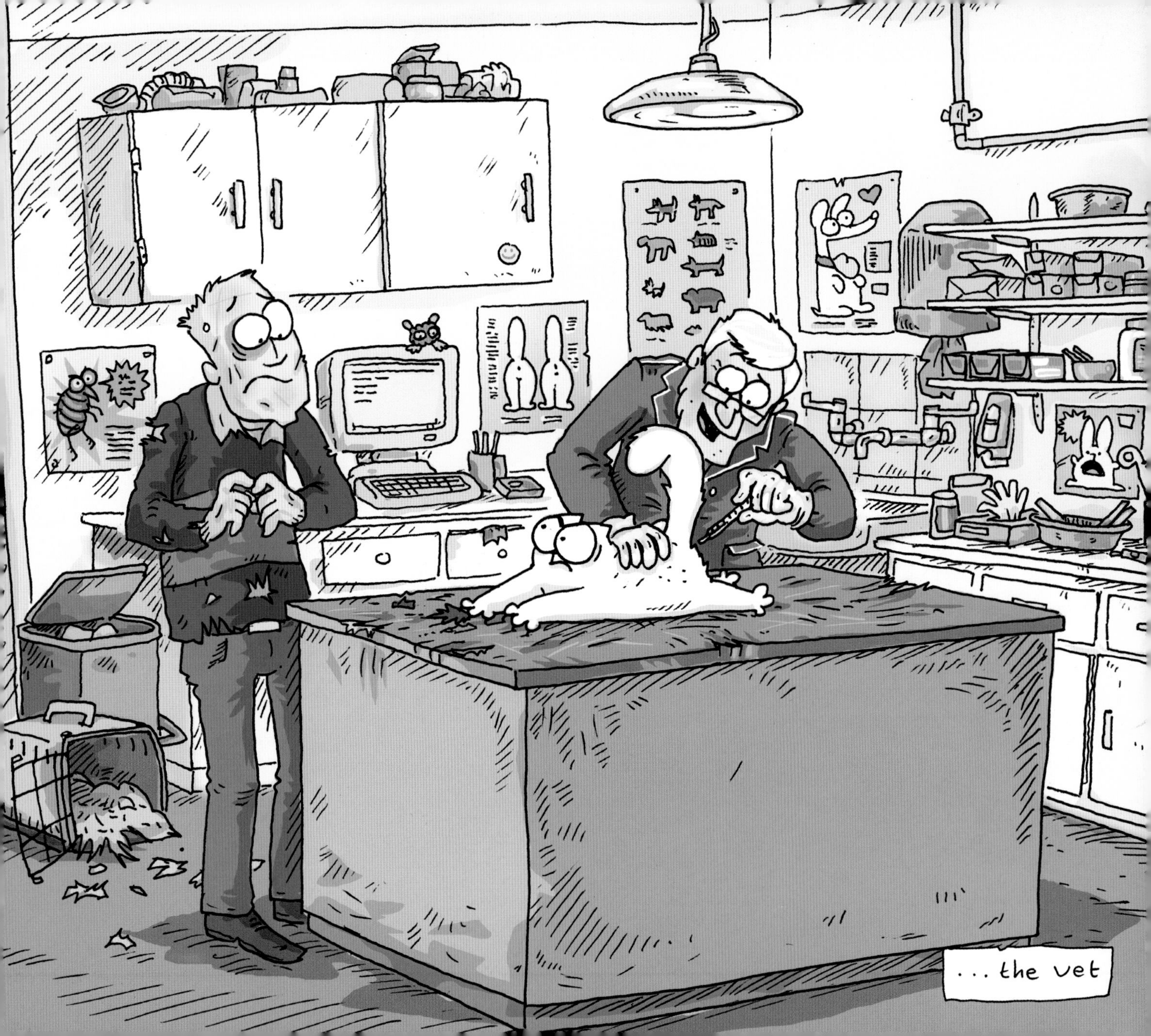
. . . the vet

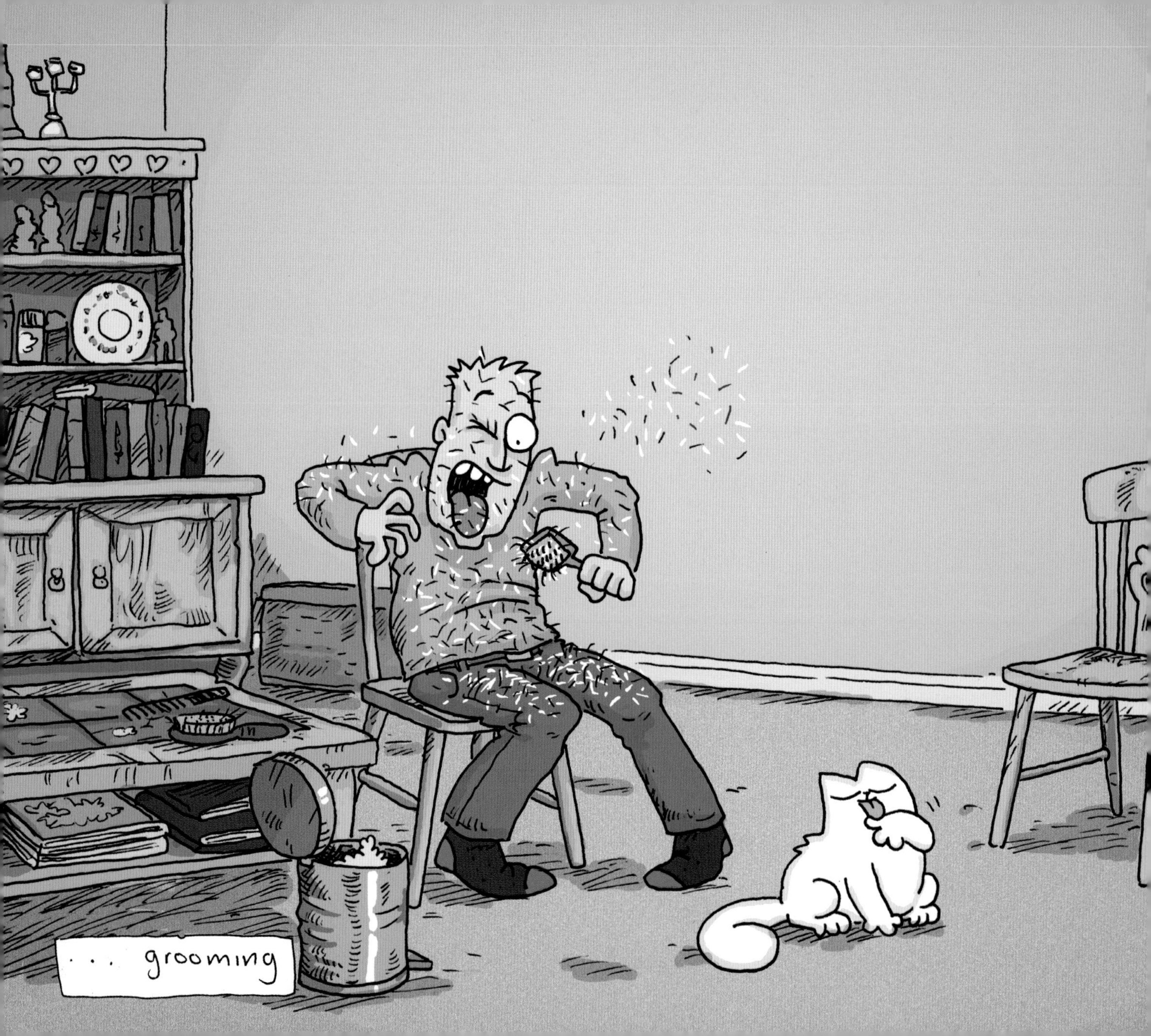
. . . grooming

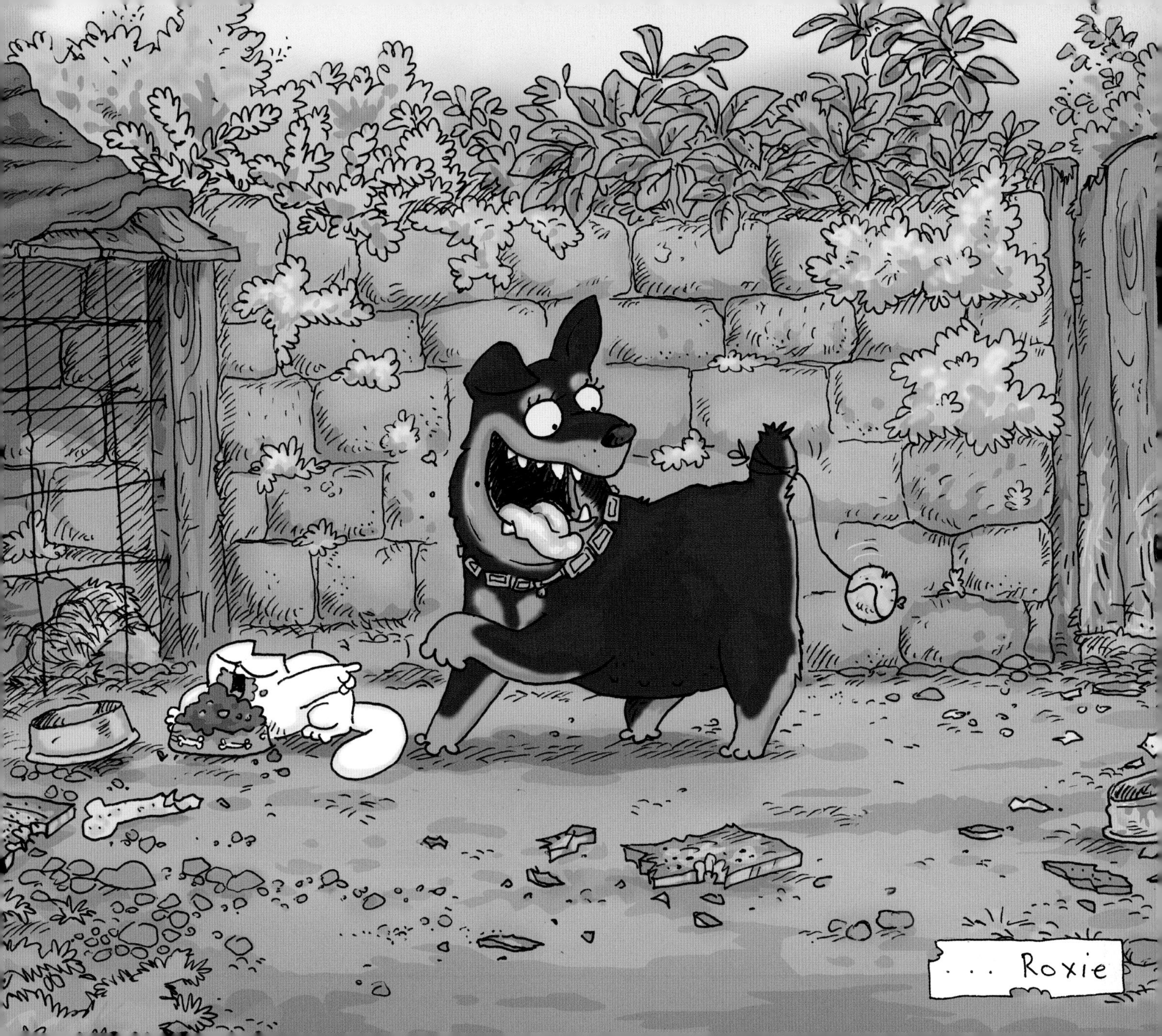
. . . Roxie

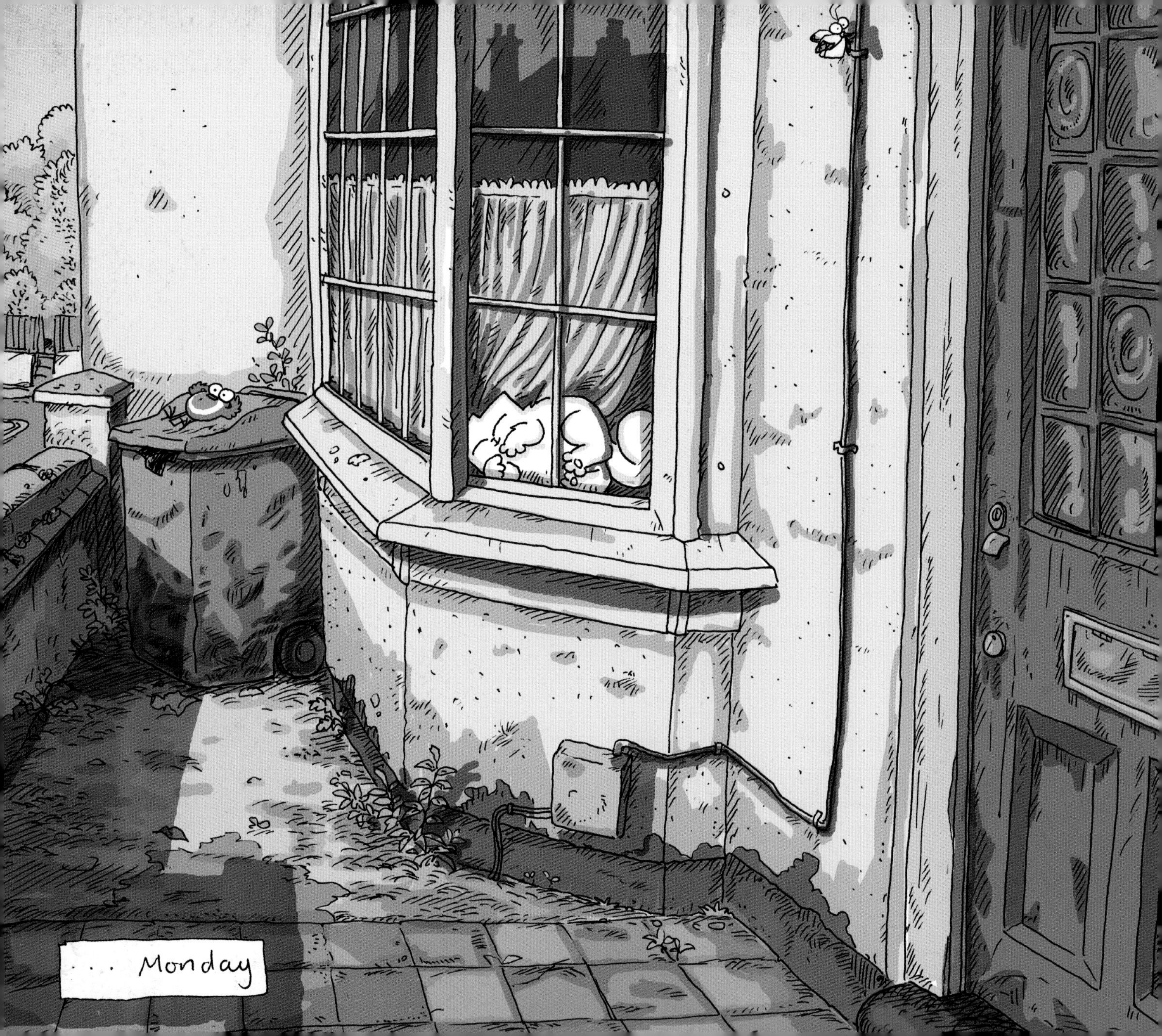
. . . Monday

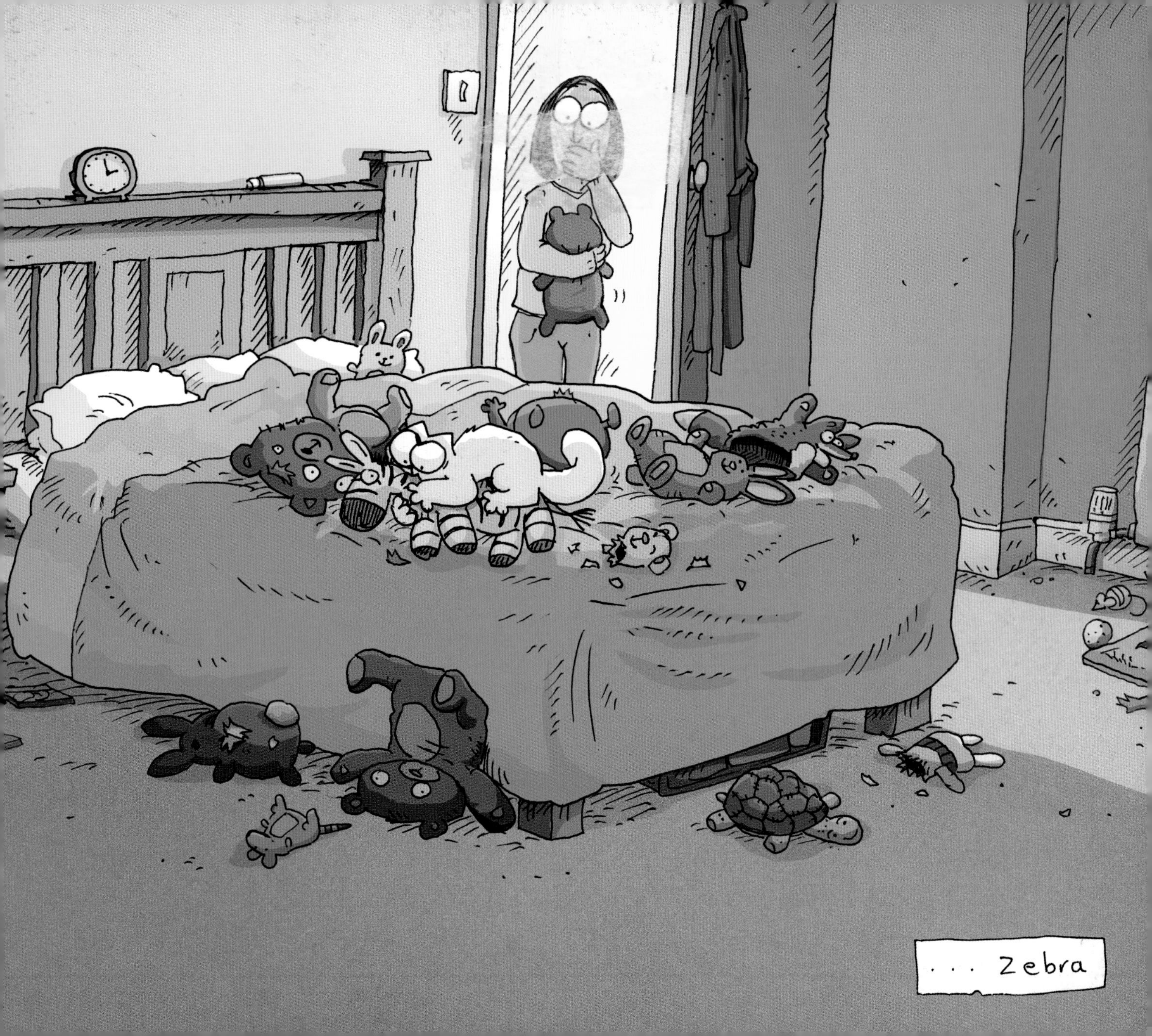
. . . Zebra

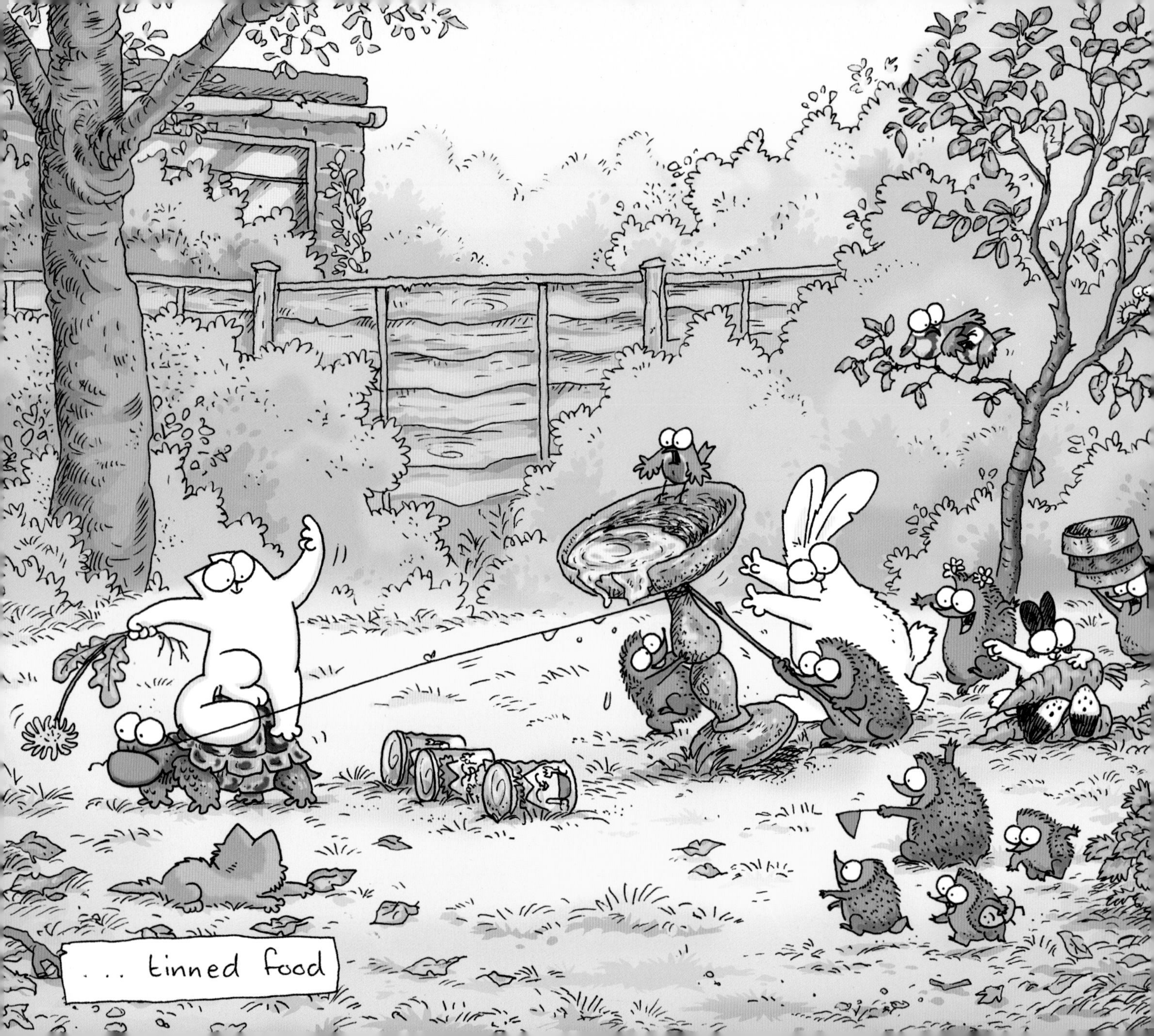
. . . tinned food

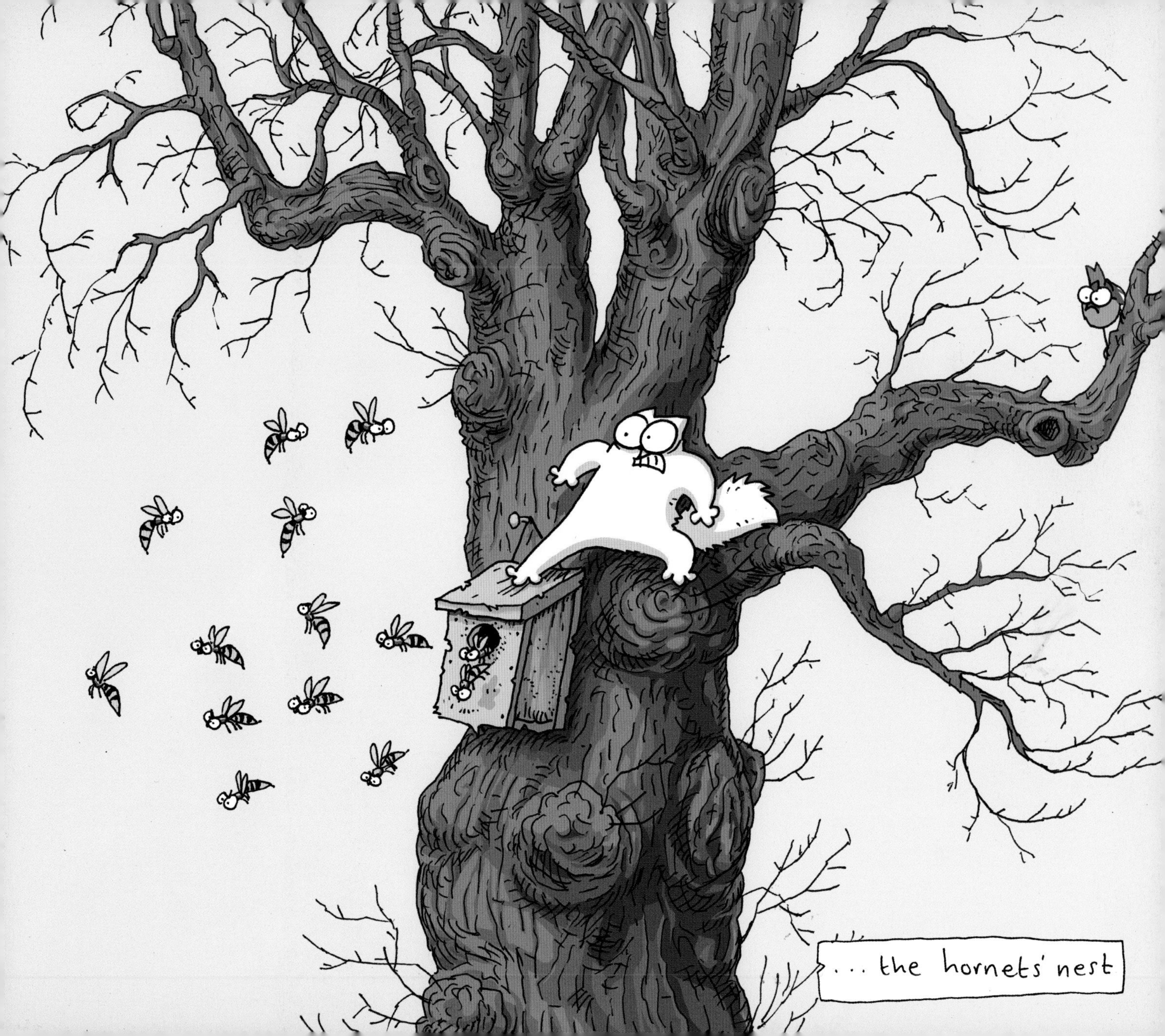
... the hornets' nest

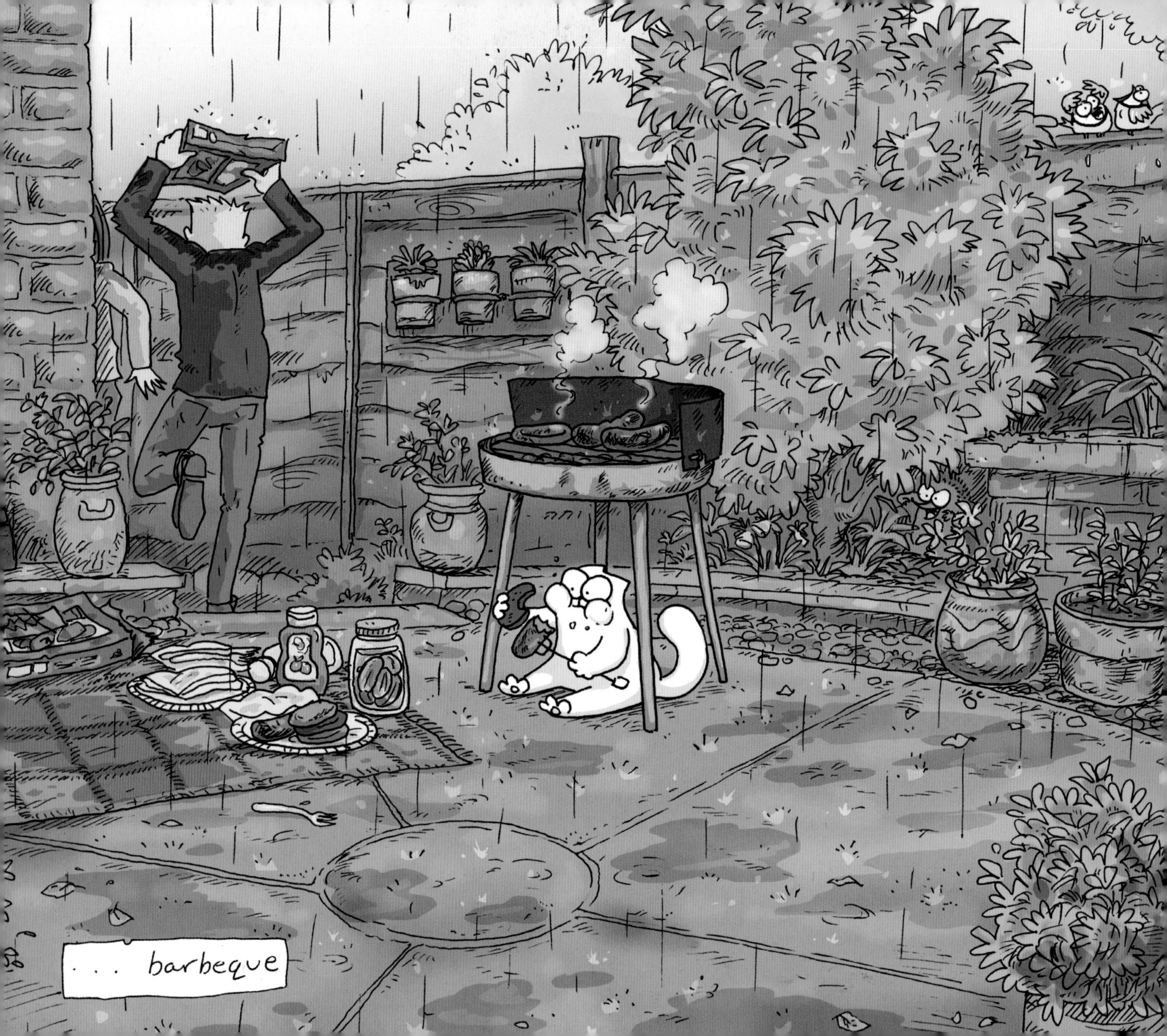
. . . barbeque

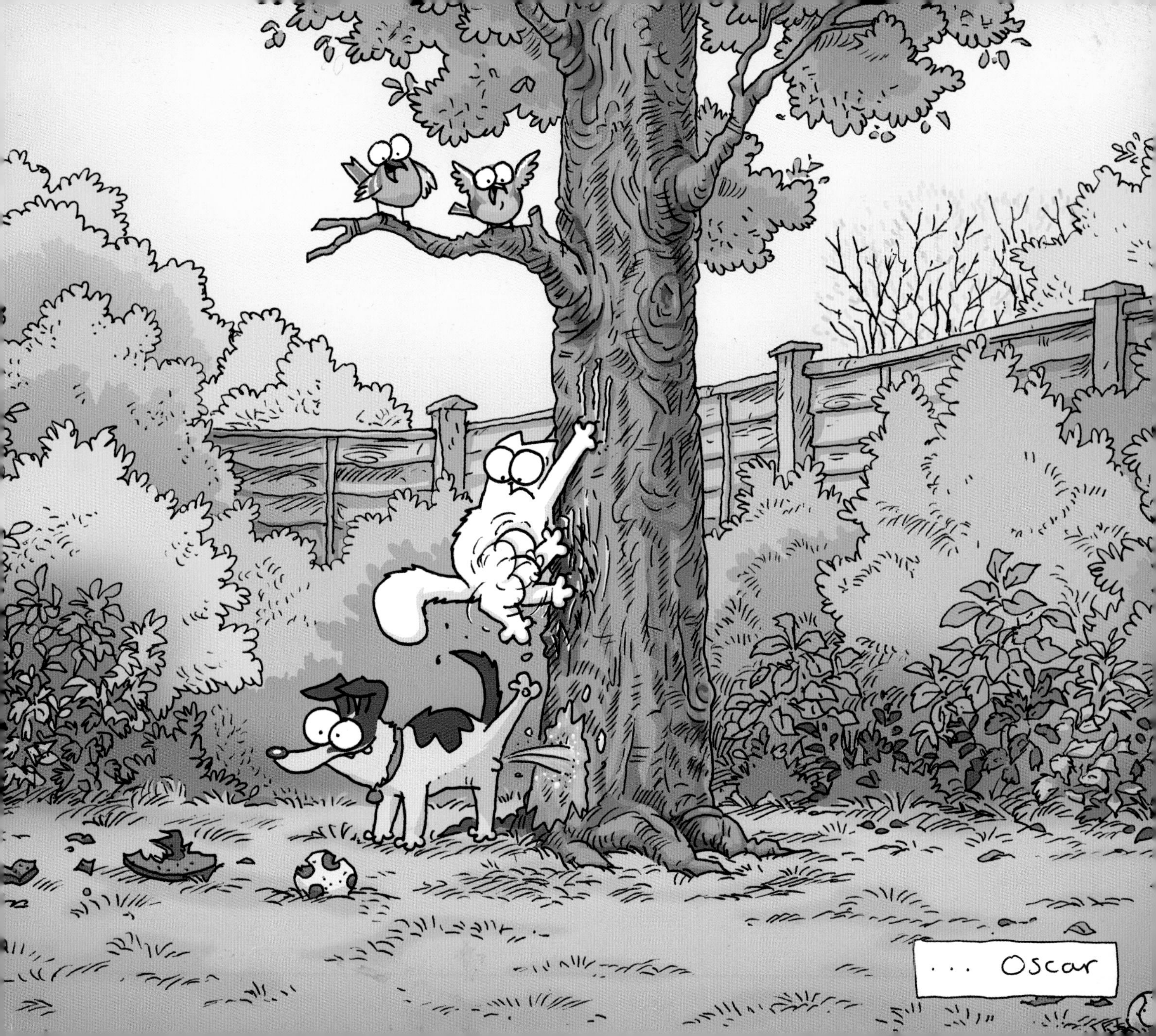
. . . Oscar

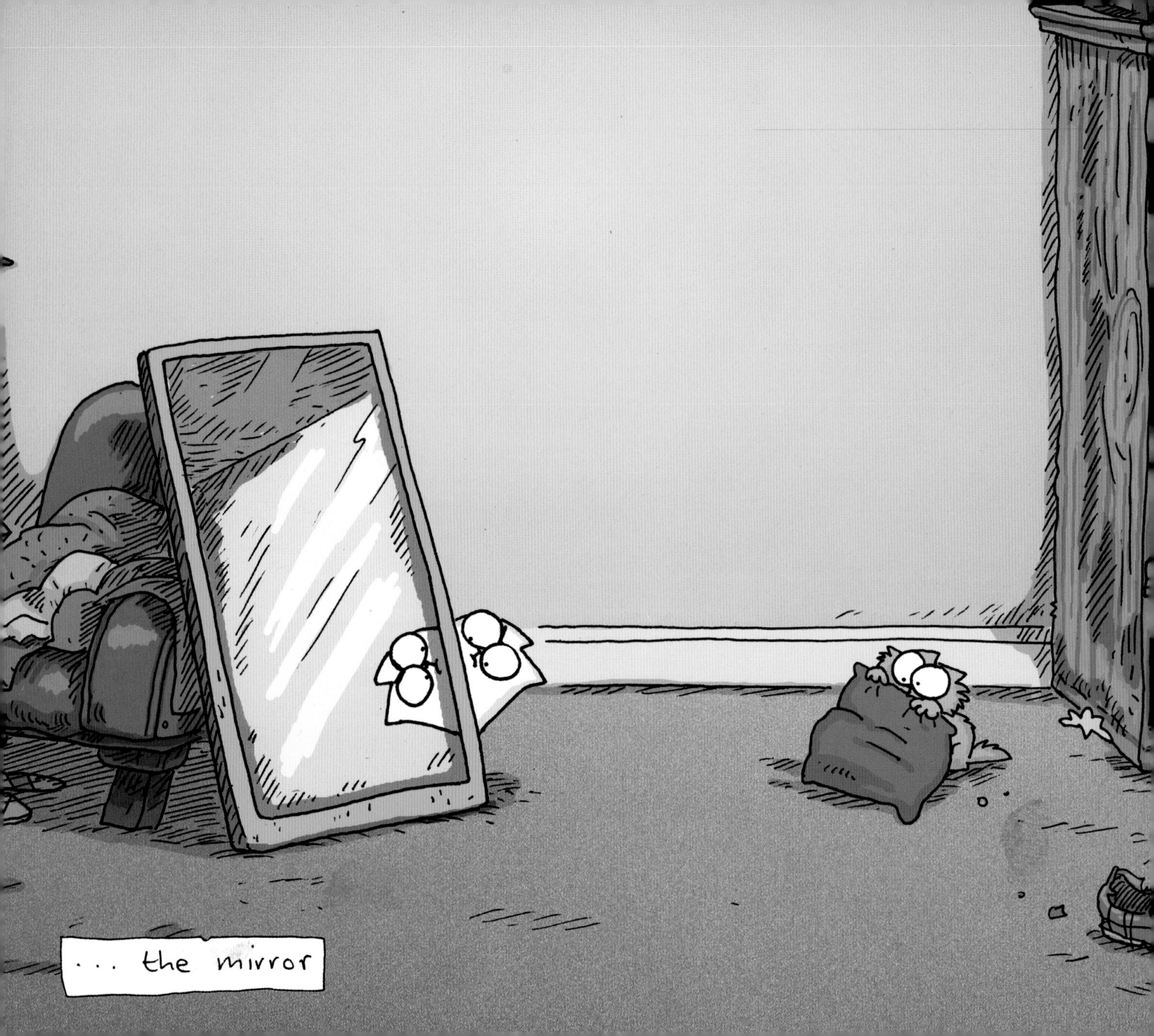
. . . the mirror

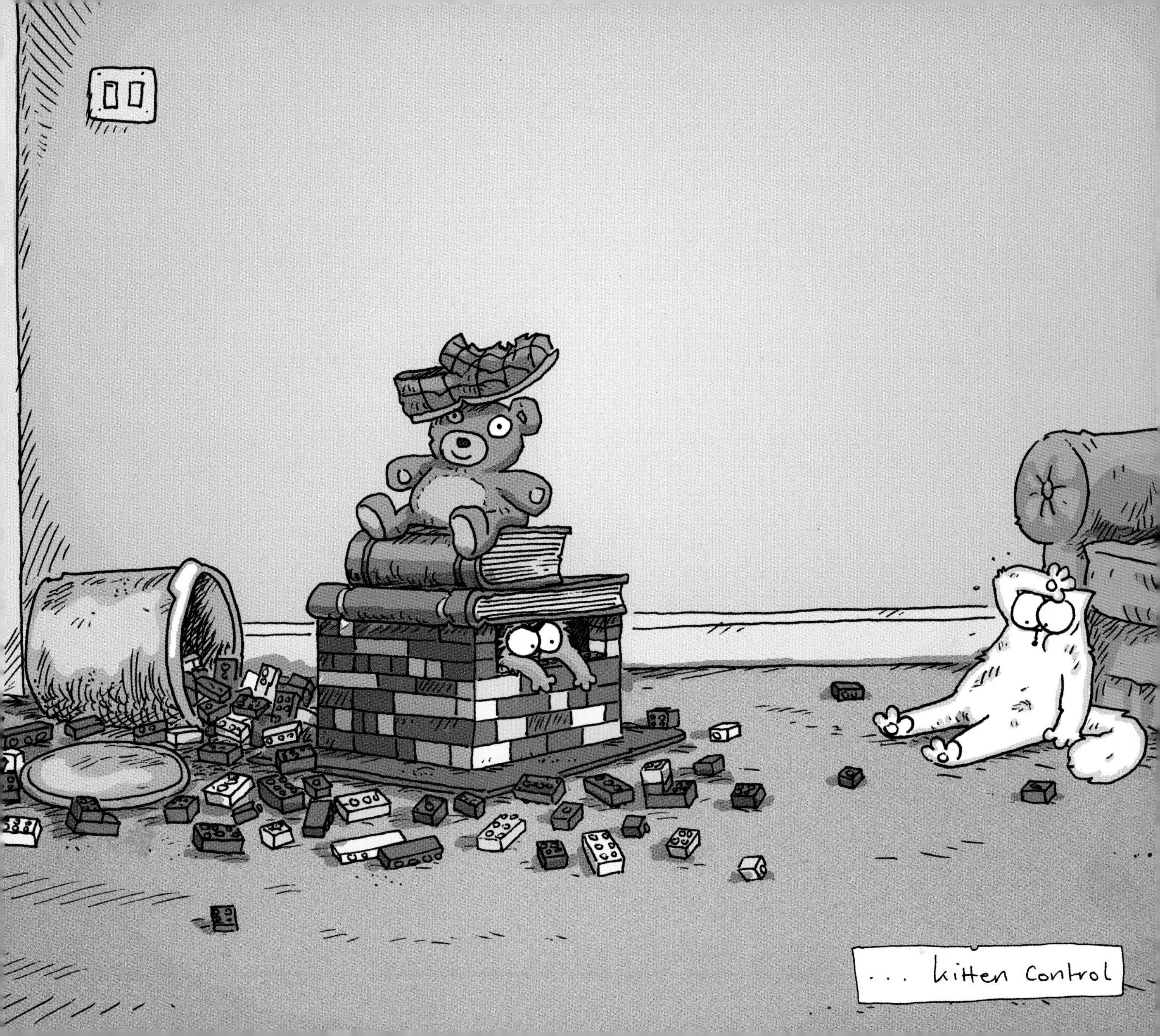
. . . kitten control

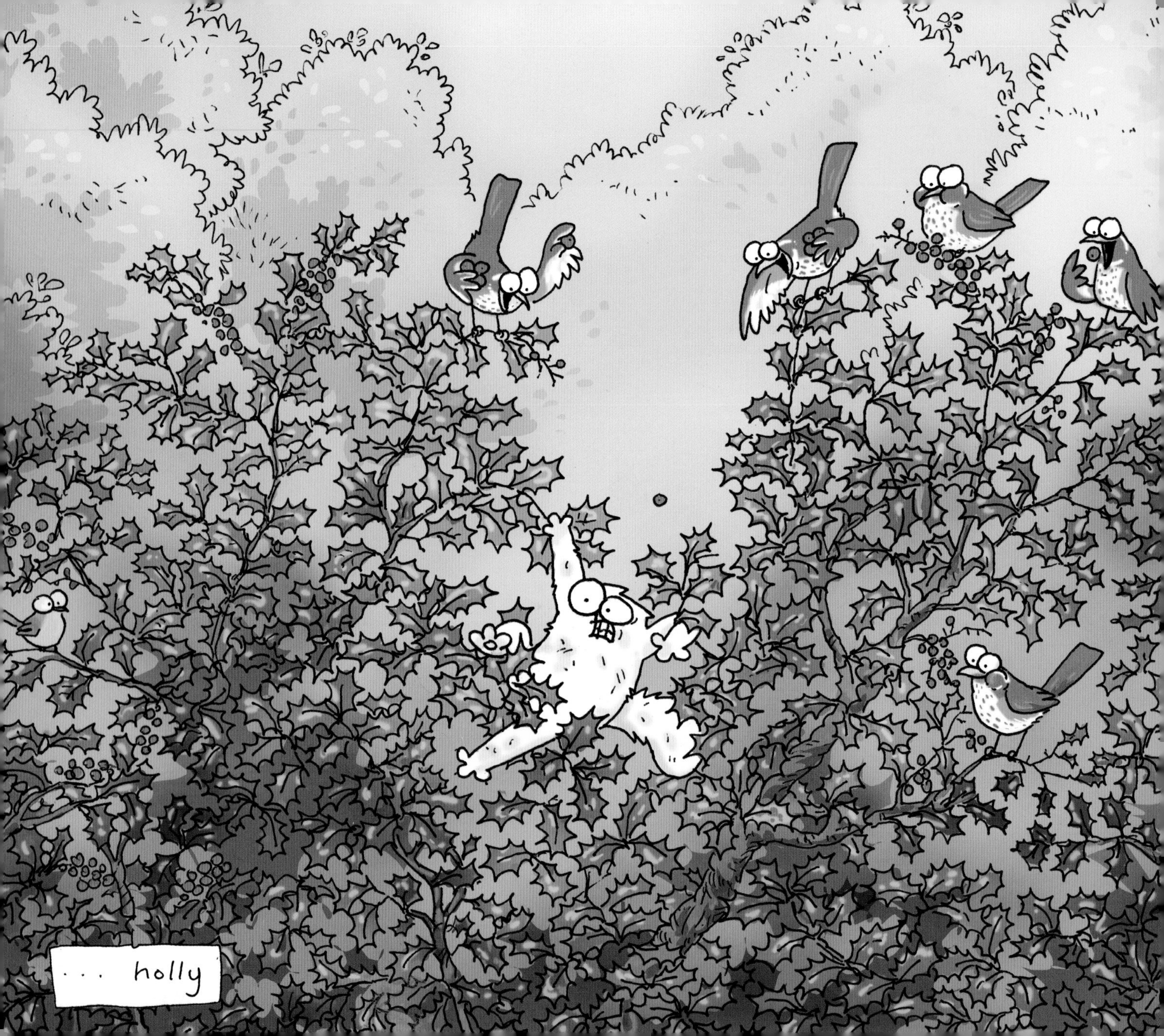
. . . holly

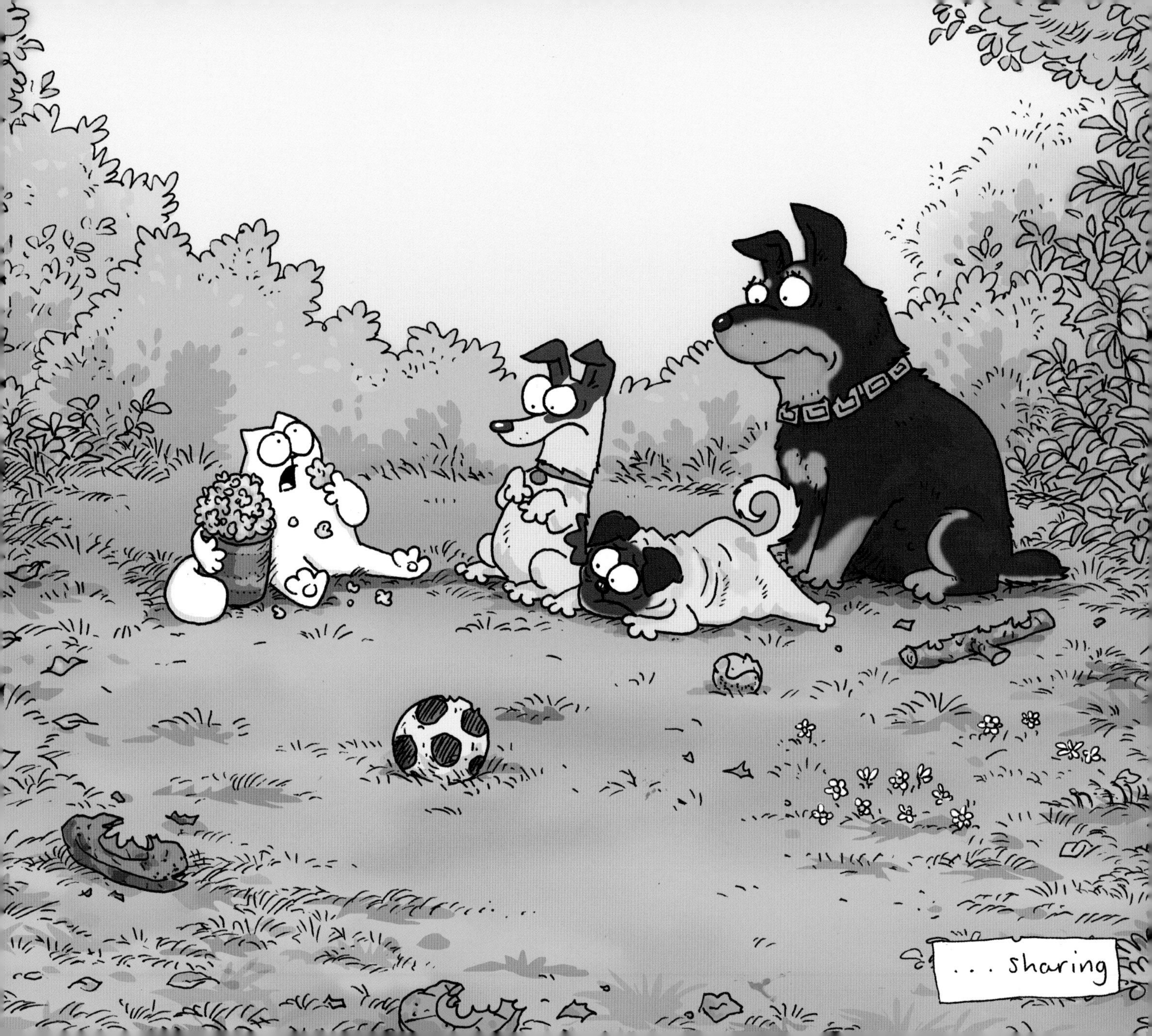
. . . sharing

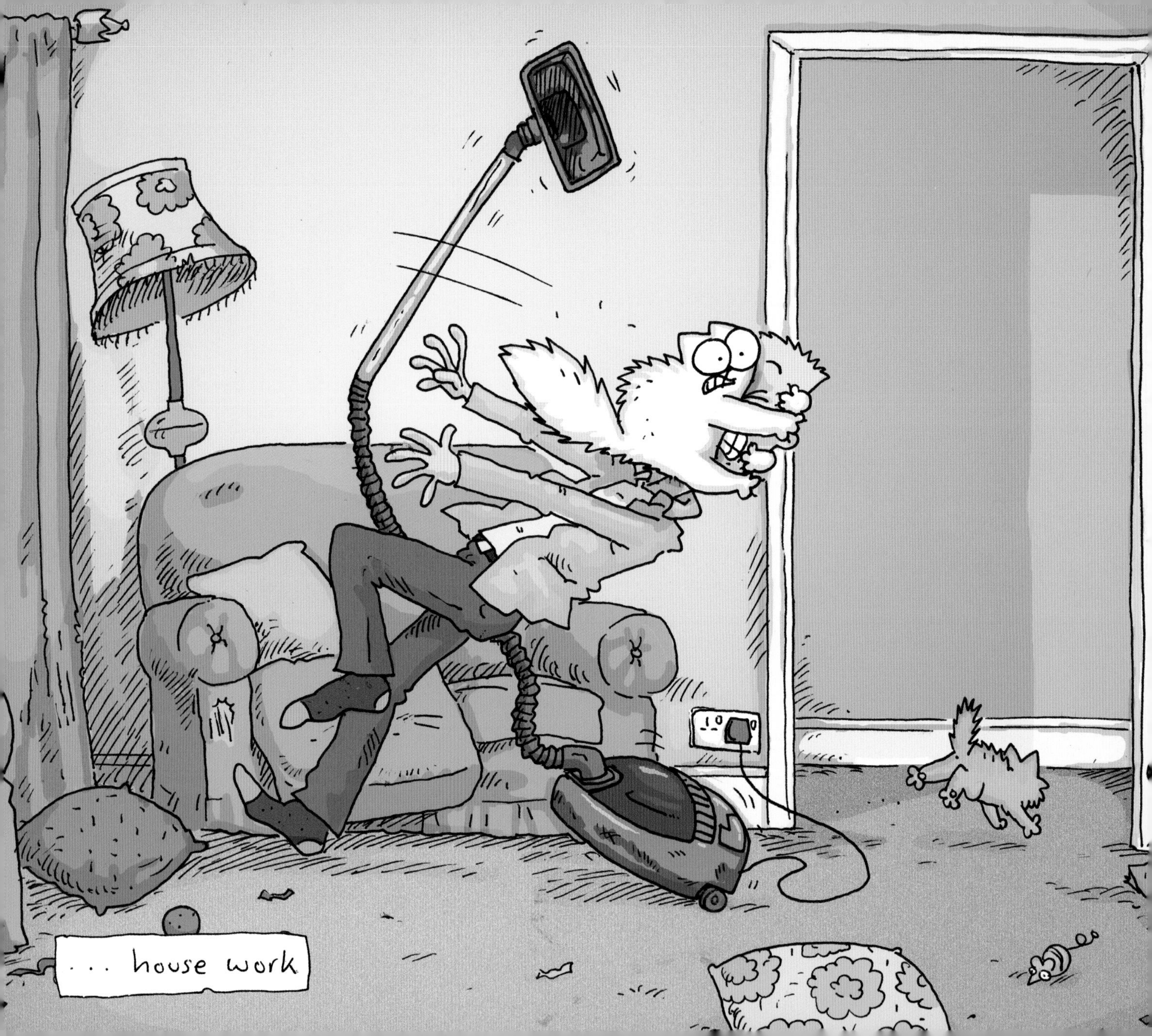
. . . house work

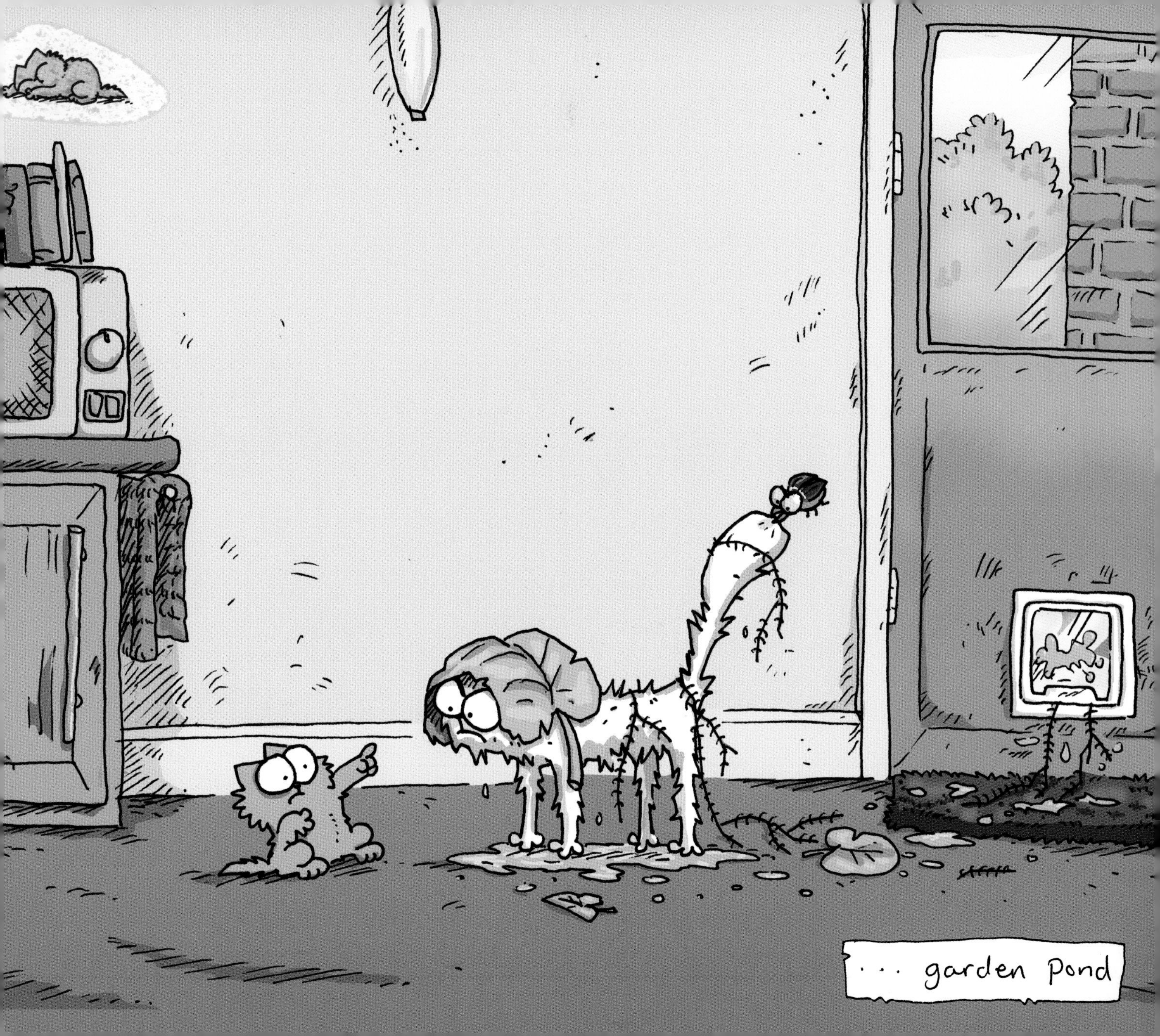
. . . garden pond

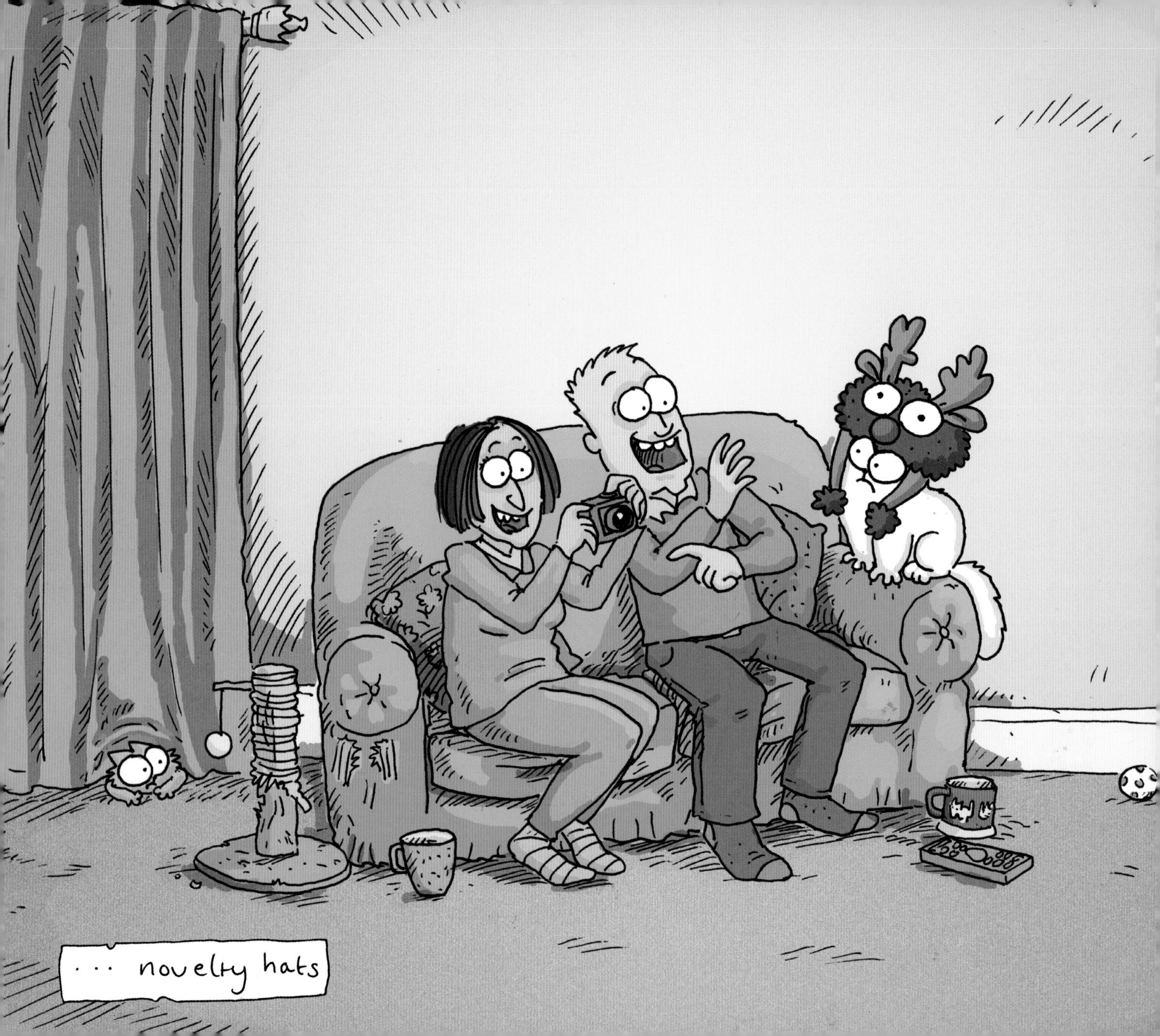
. . . novelty hats

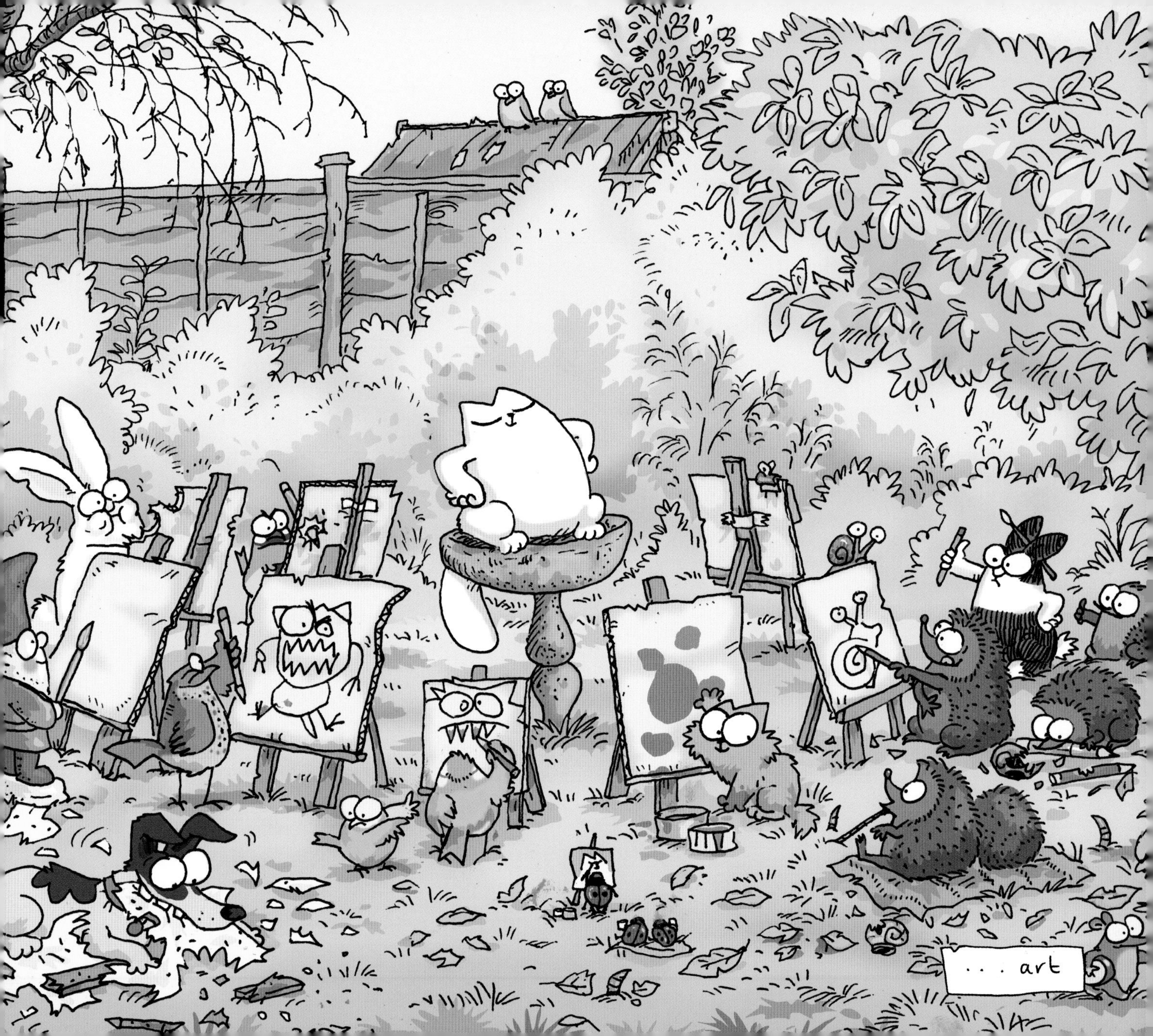
. . . art

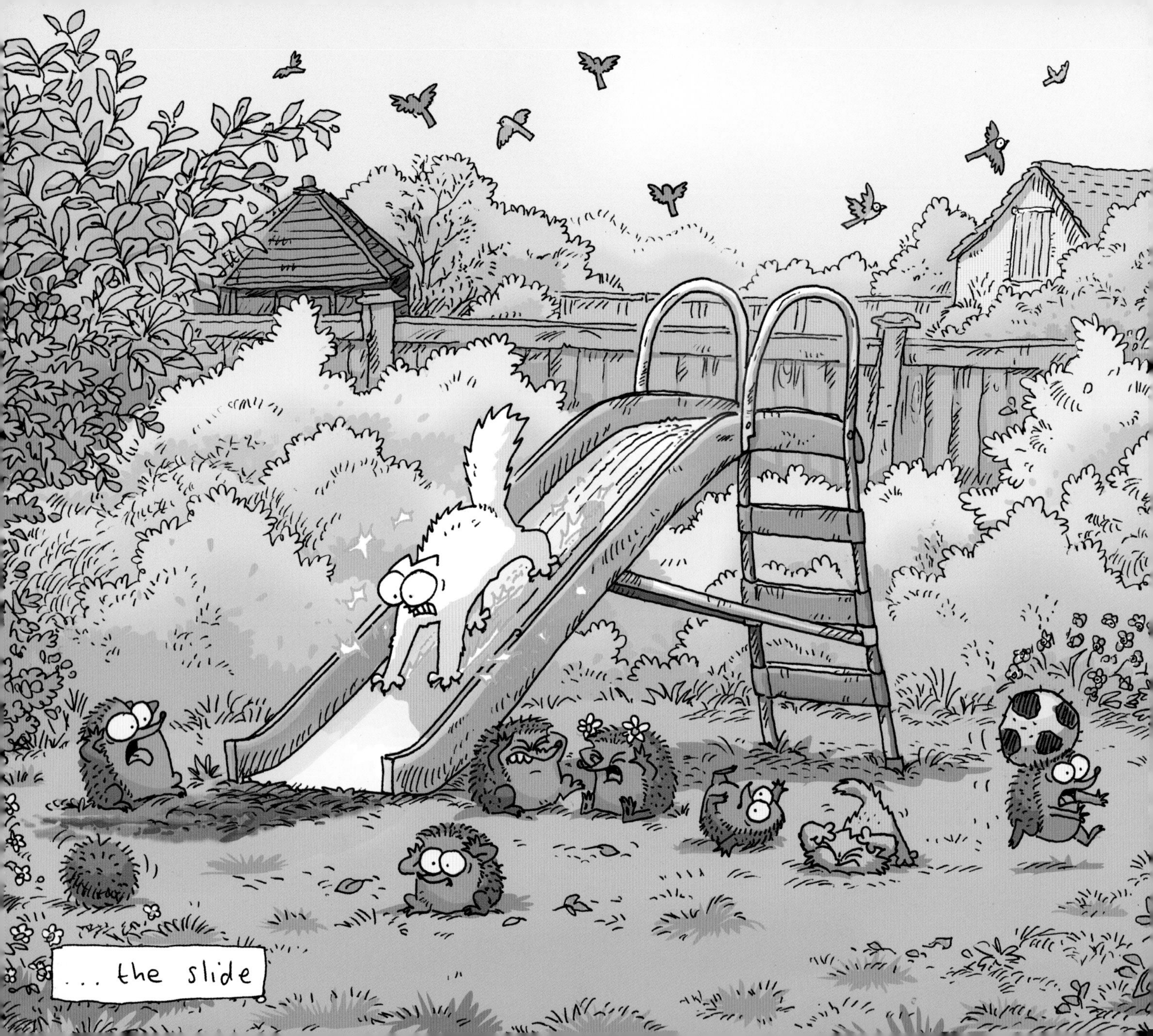
. . . the slide

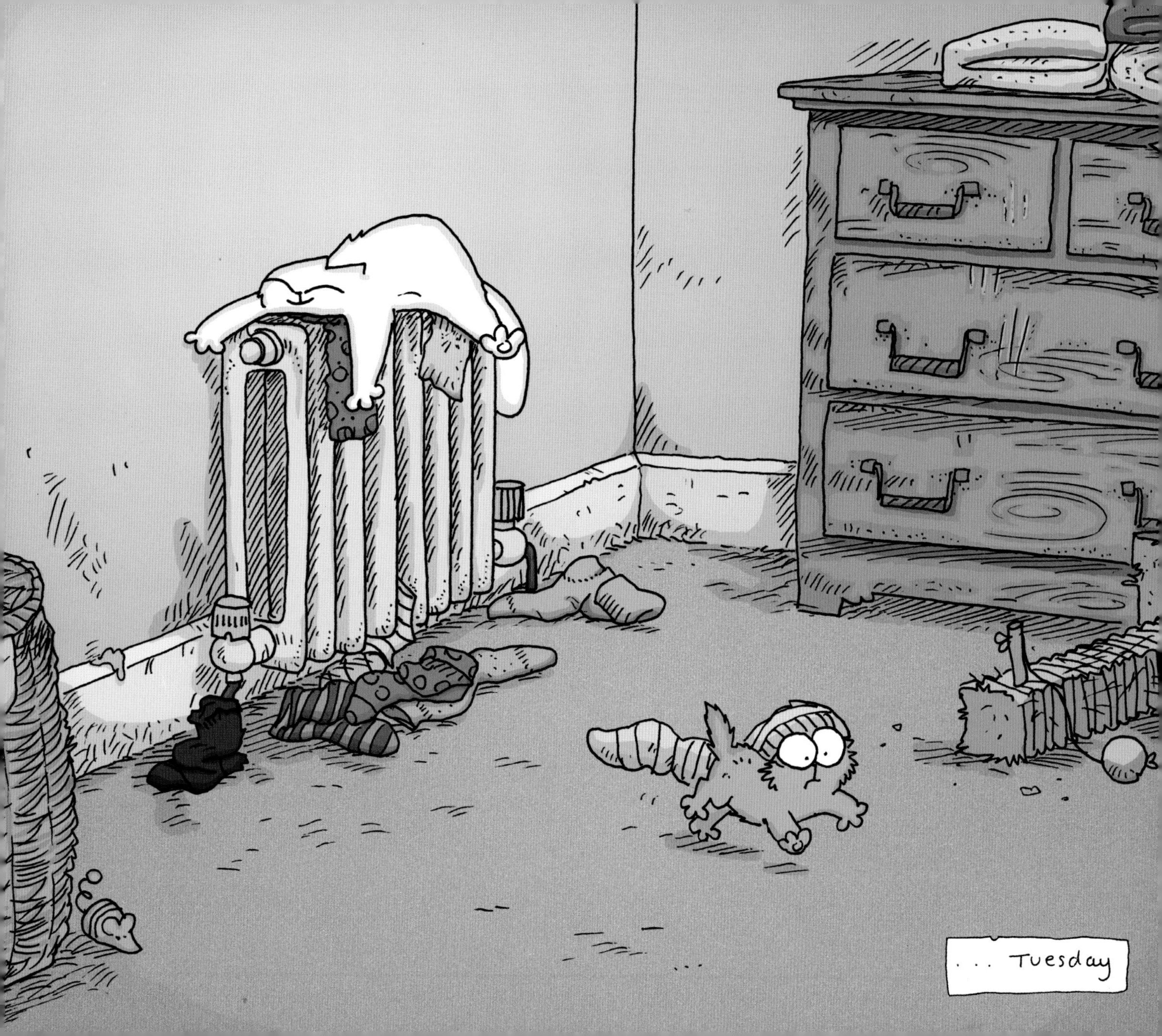
. . . Tuesday

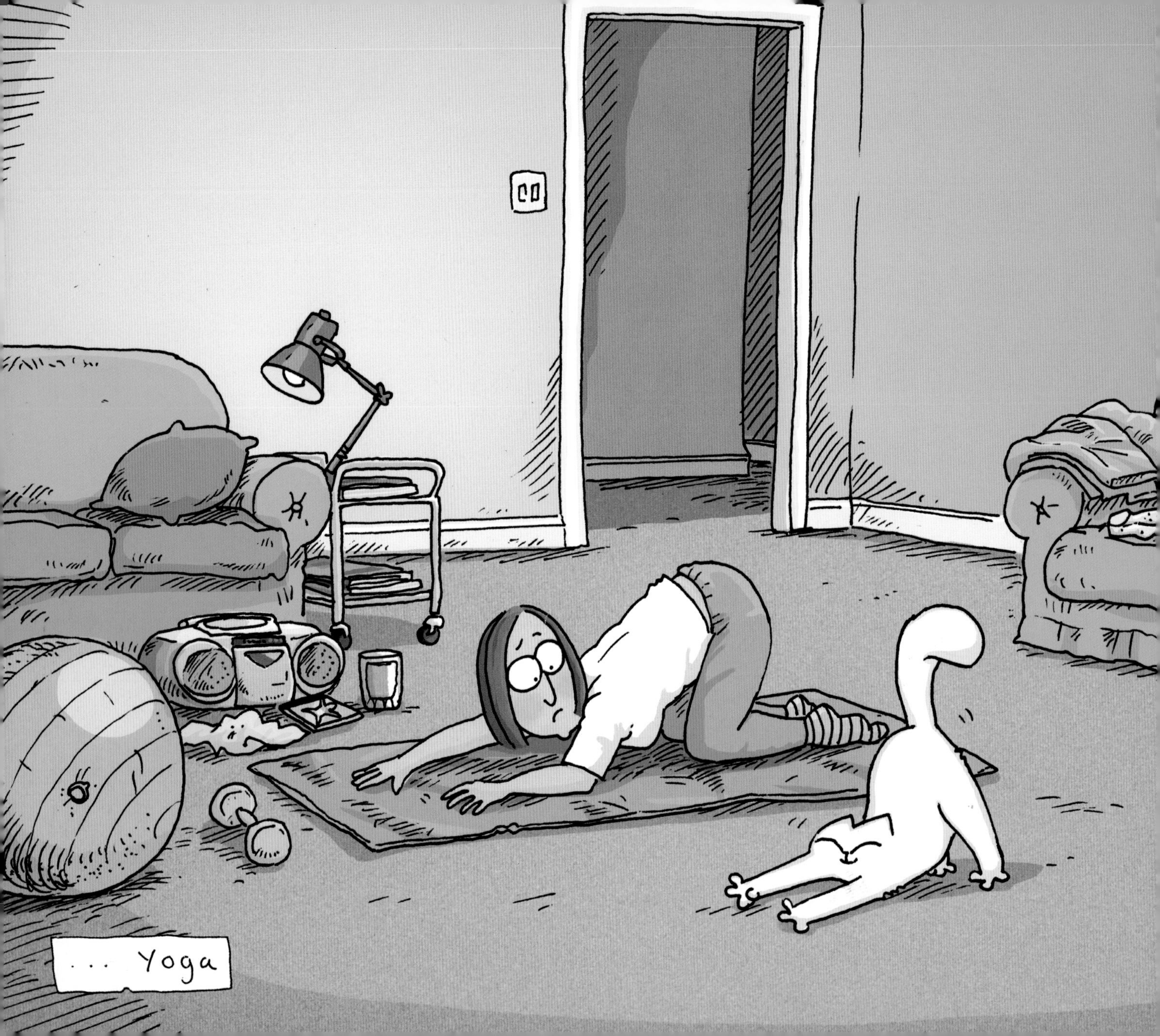
. . . Yoga

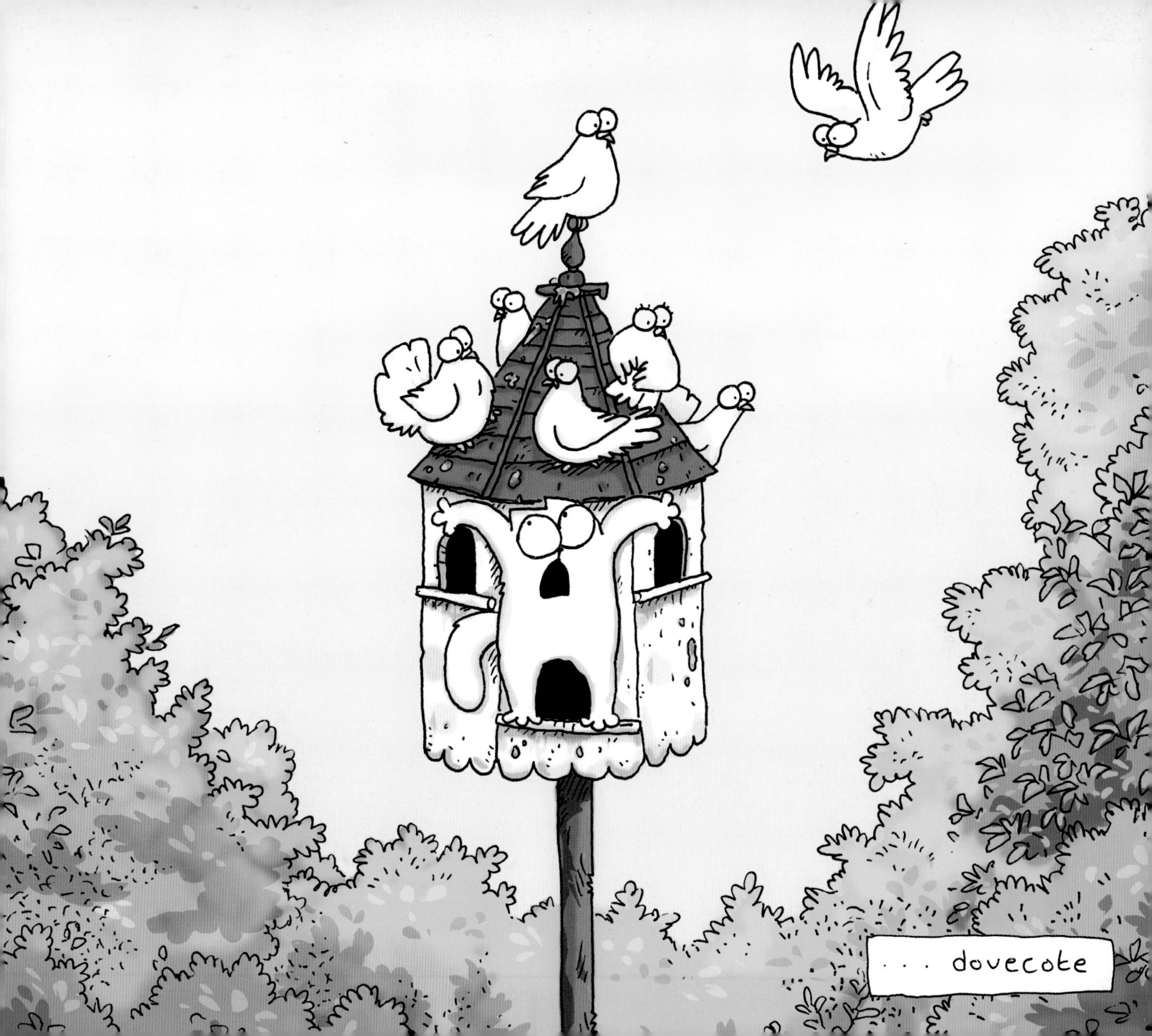
. . . dovecote

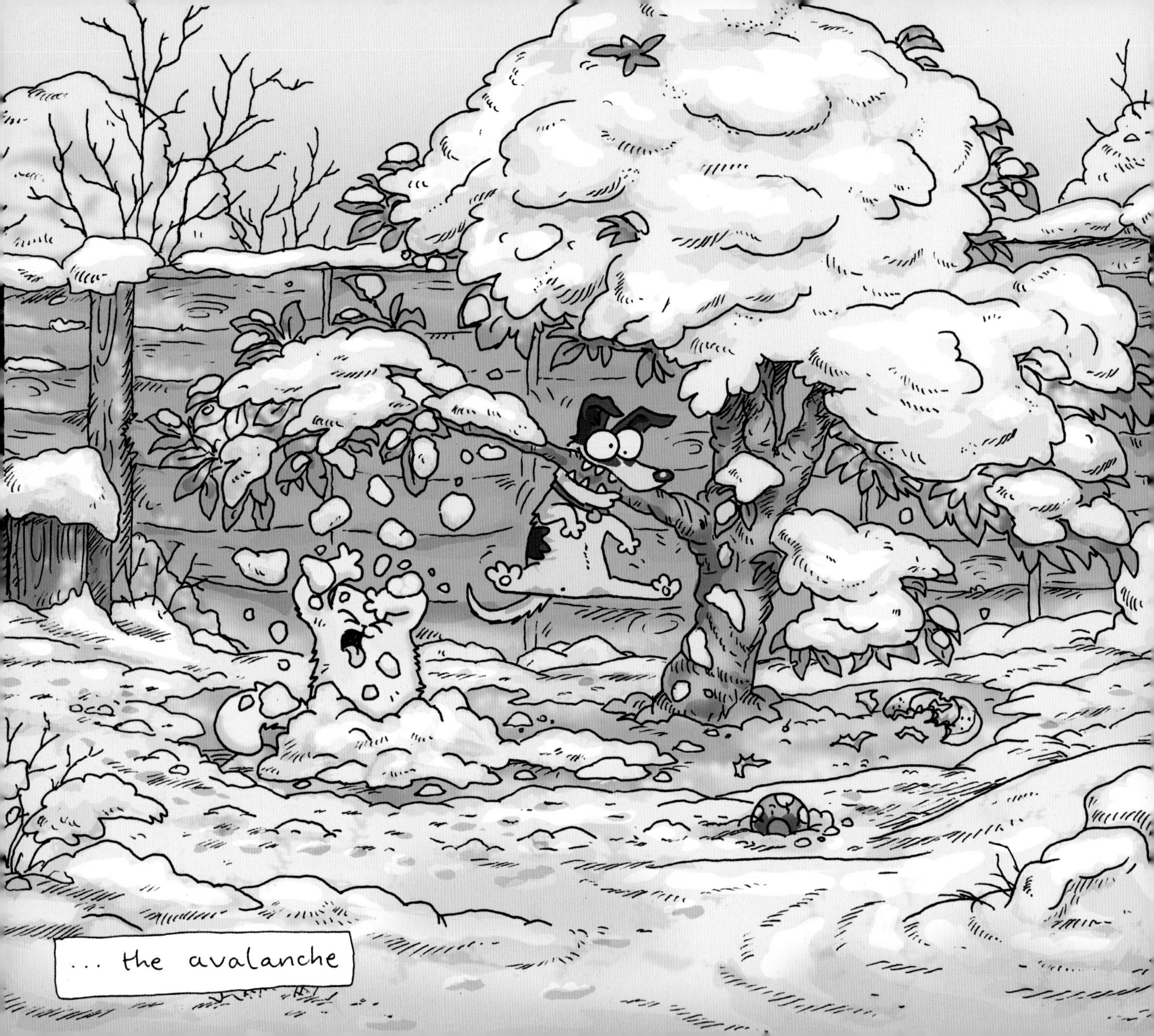
... the avalanche

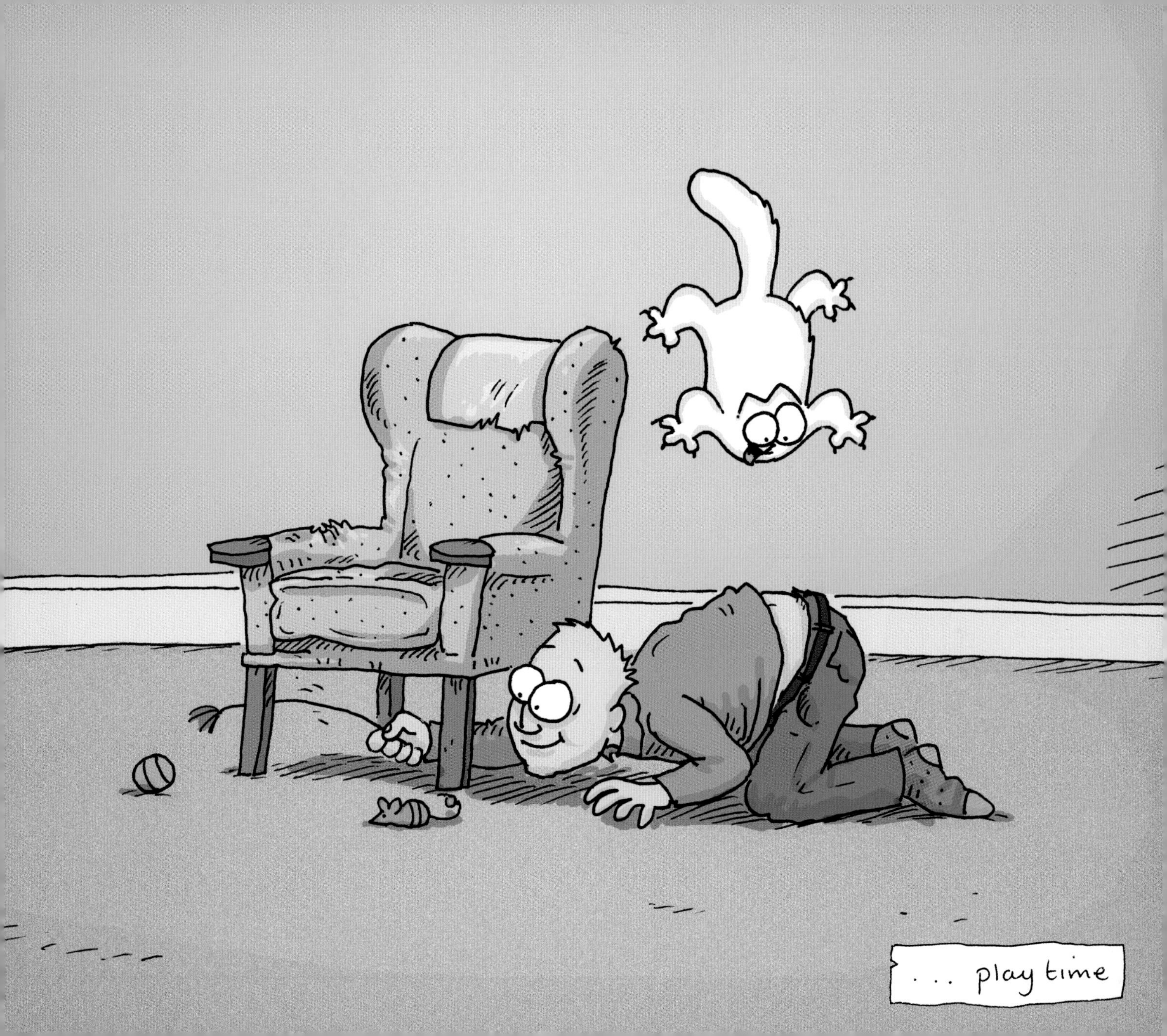
. . . play time

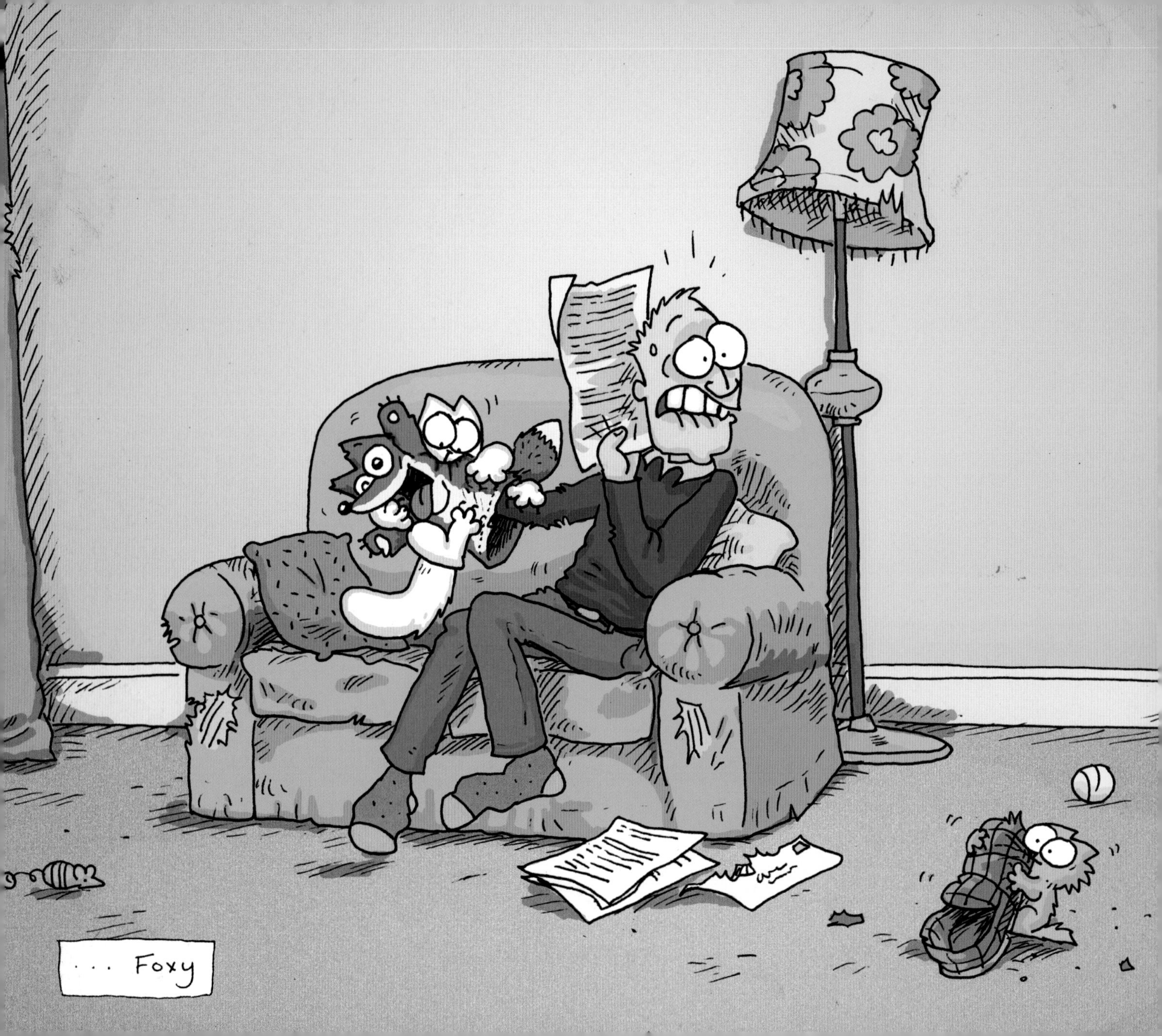
. . . Foxy

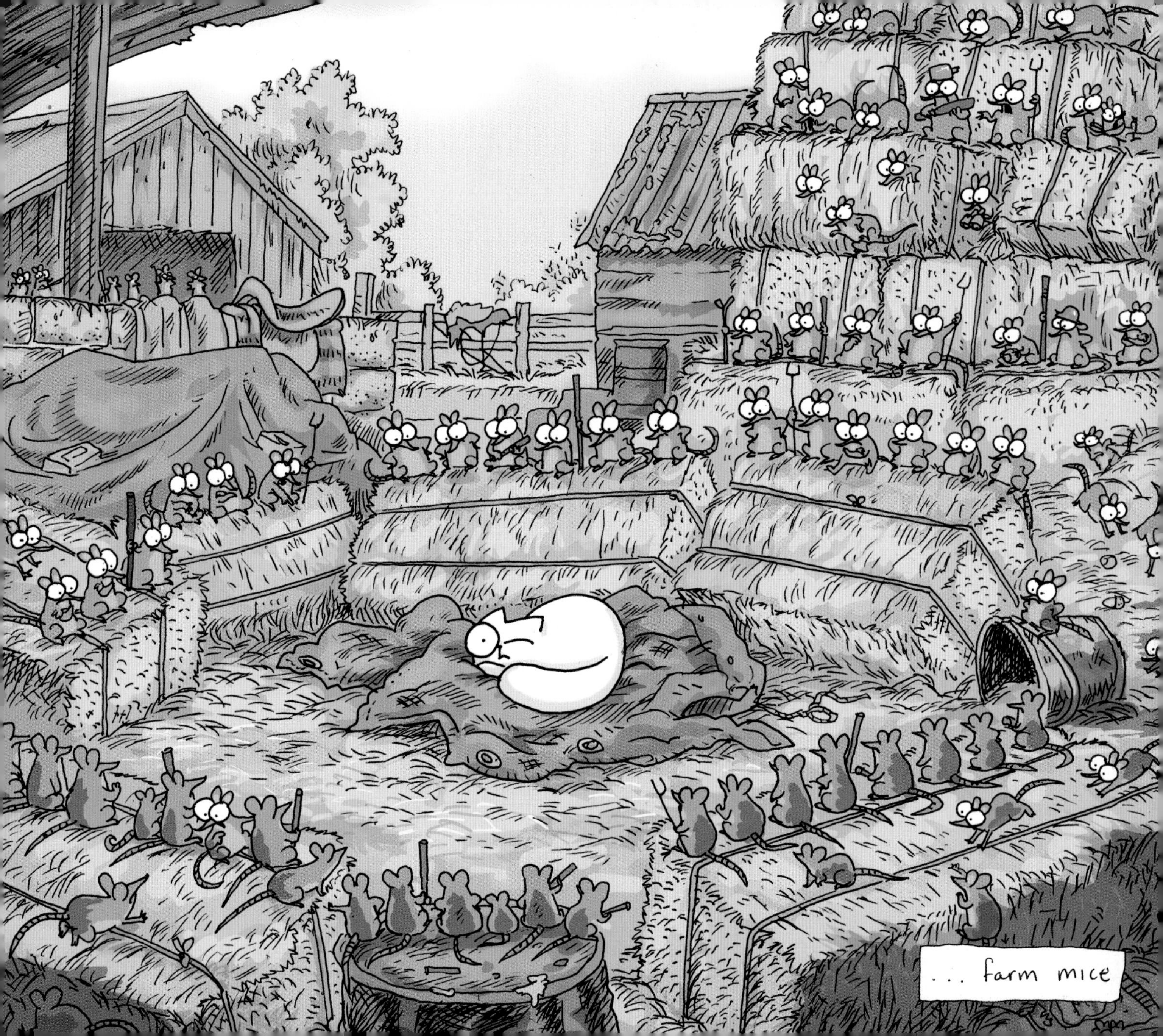
. . . farm mice

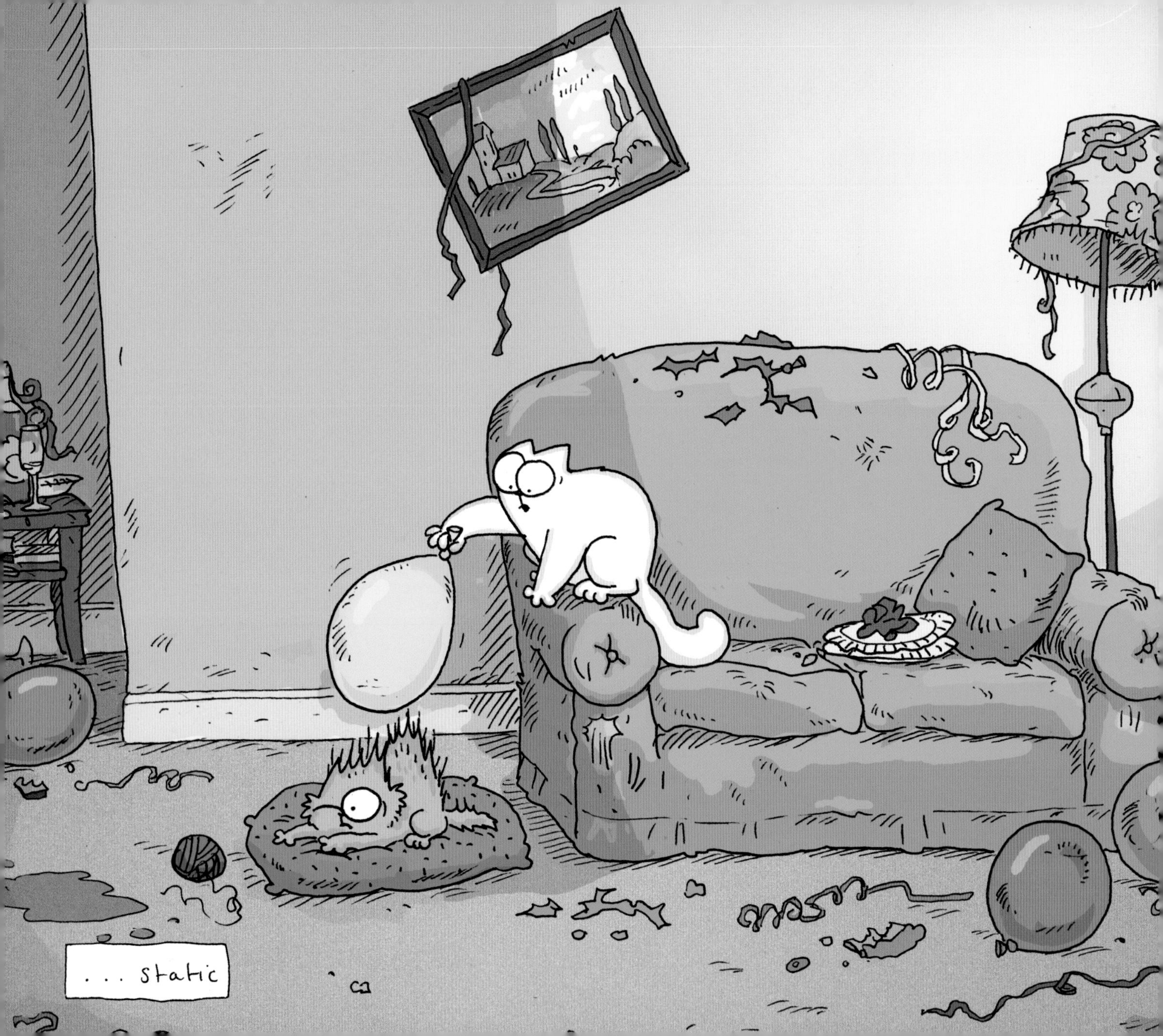
. . . static

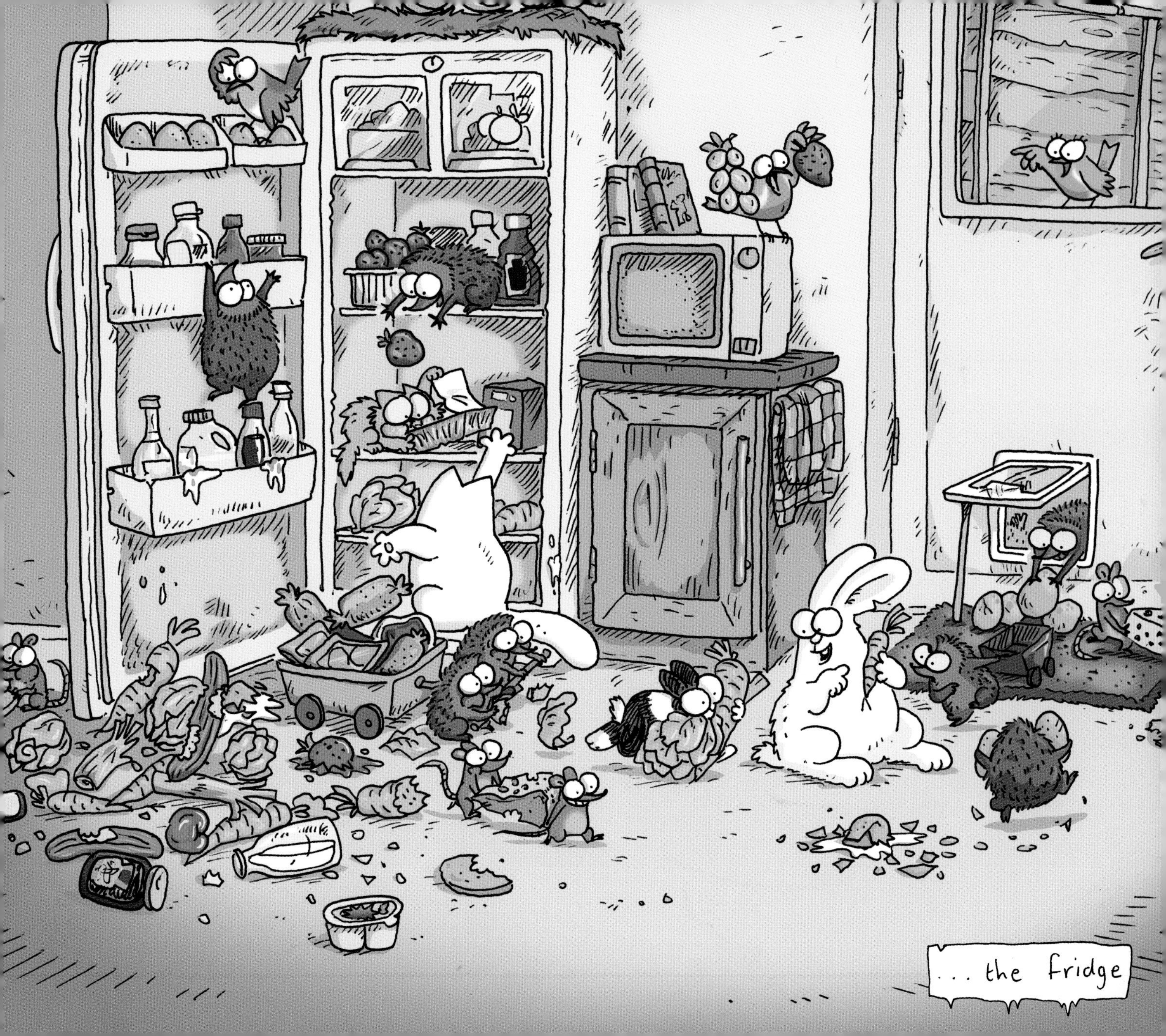
. . . the fridge

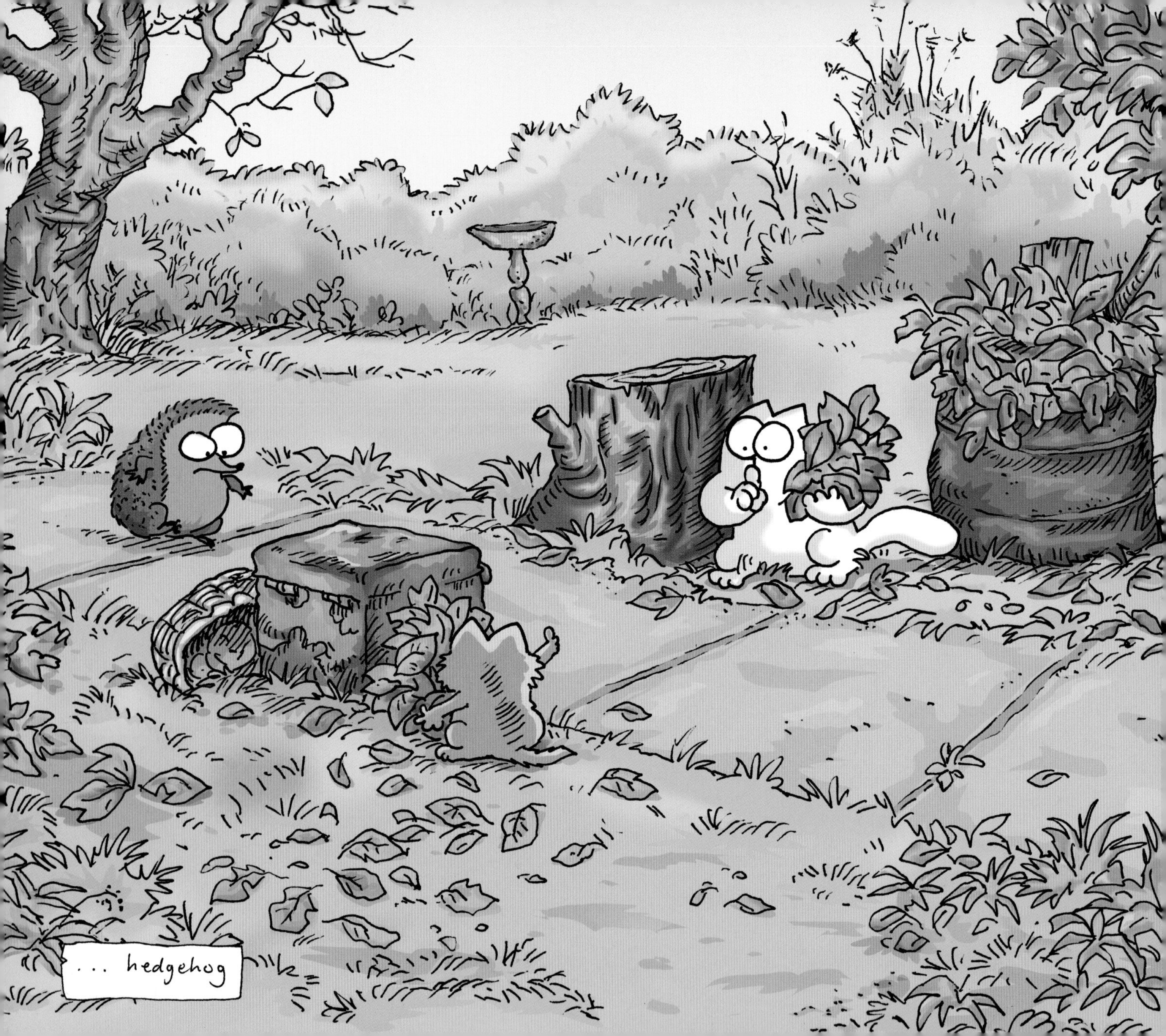
... hedgehog

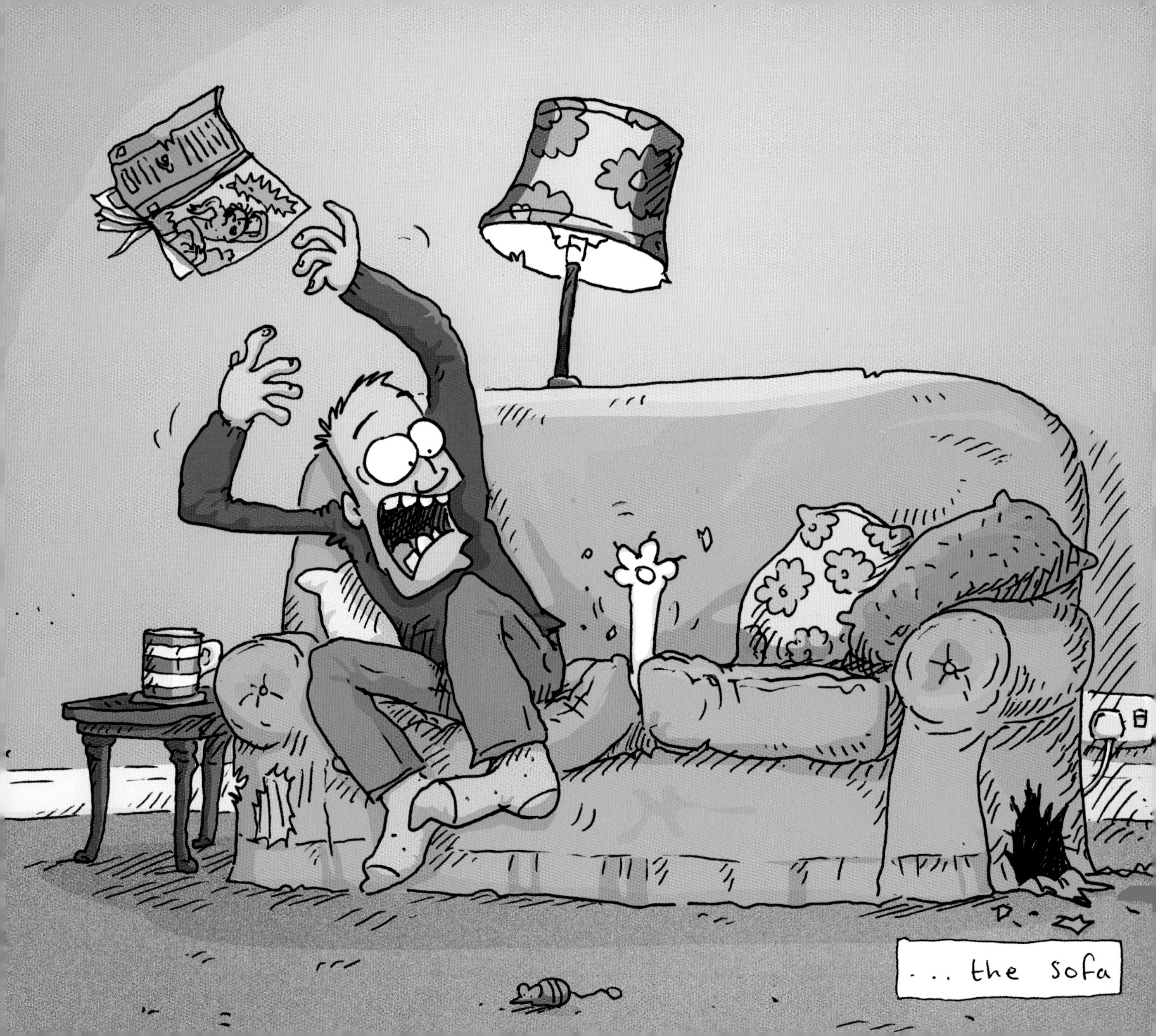
. . . the sofa

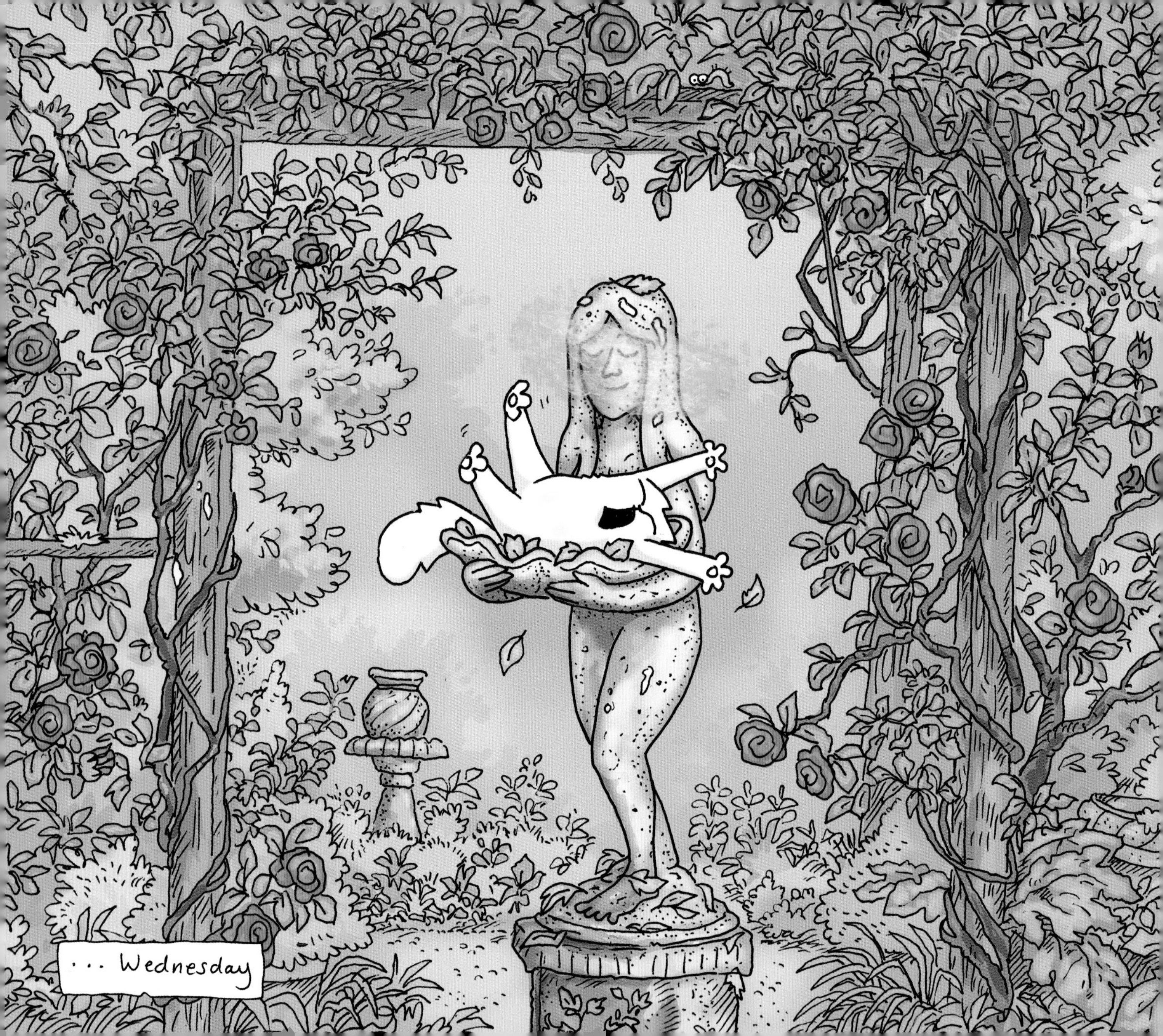
. . . Wednesday

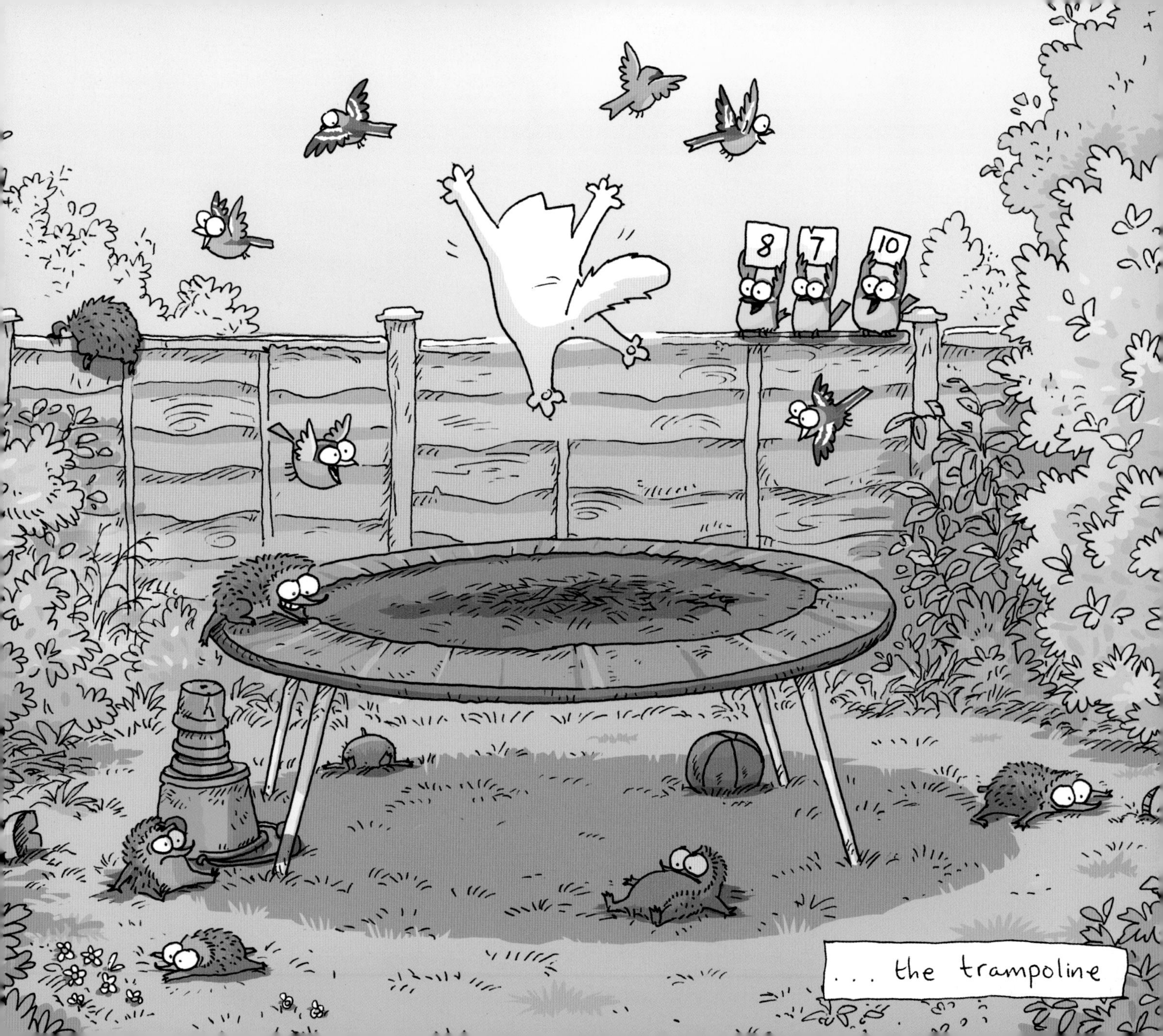
8
7
10
. . . the trampoline

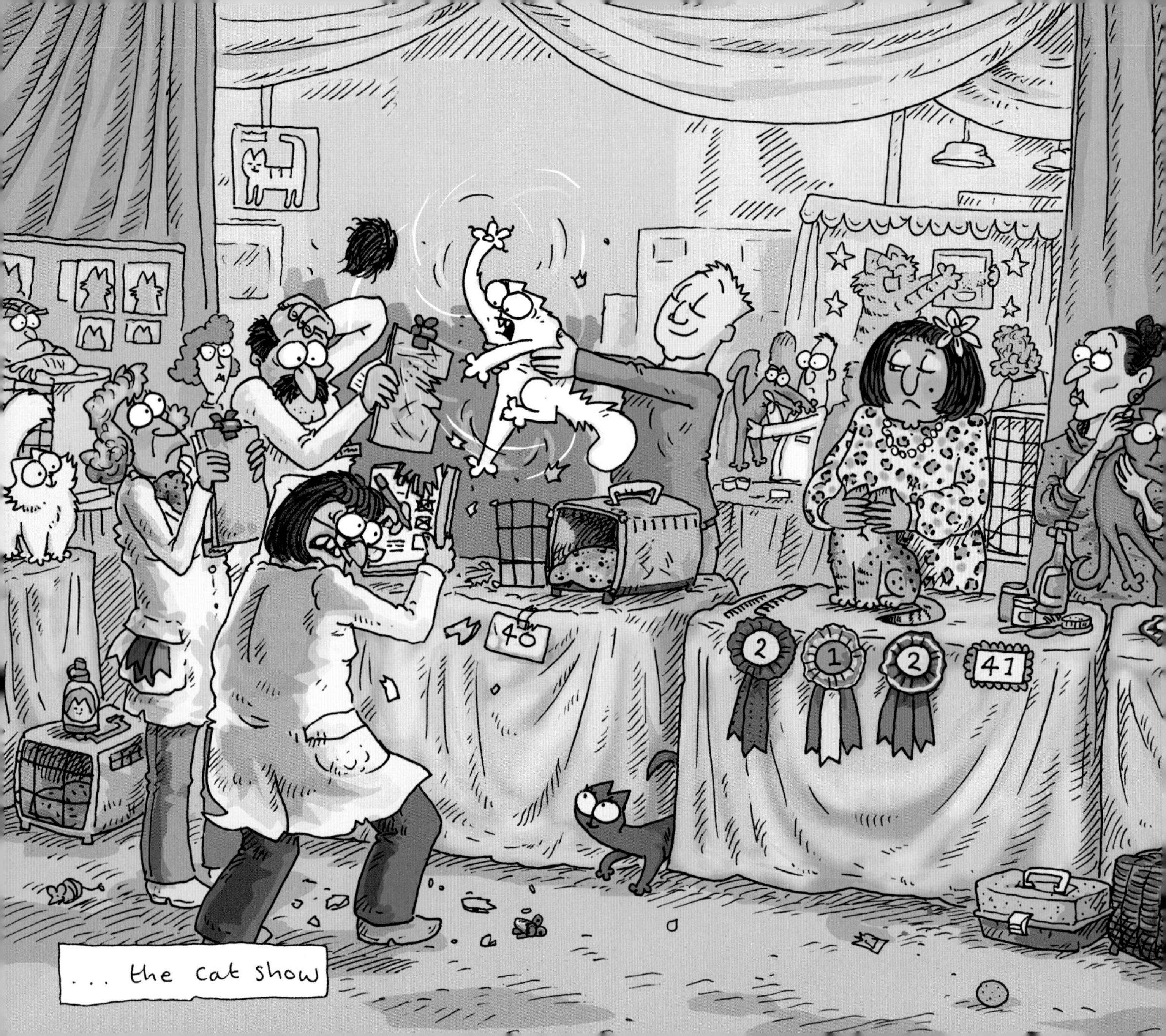
. . . the cat show
40
2
1
2
41

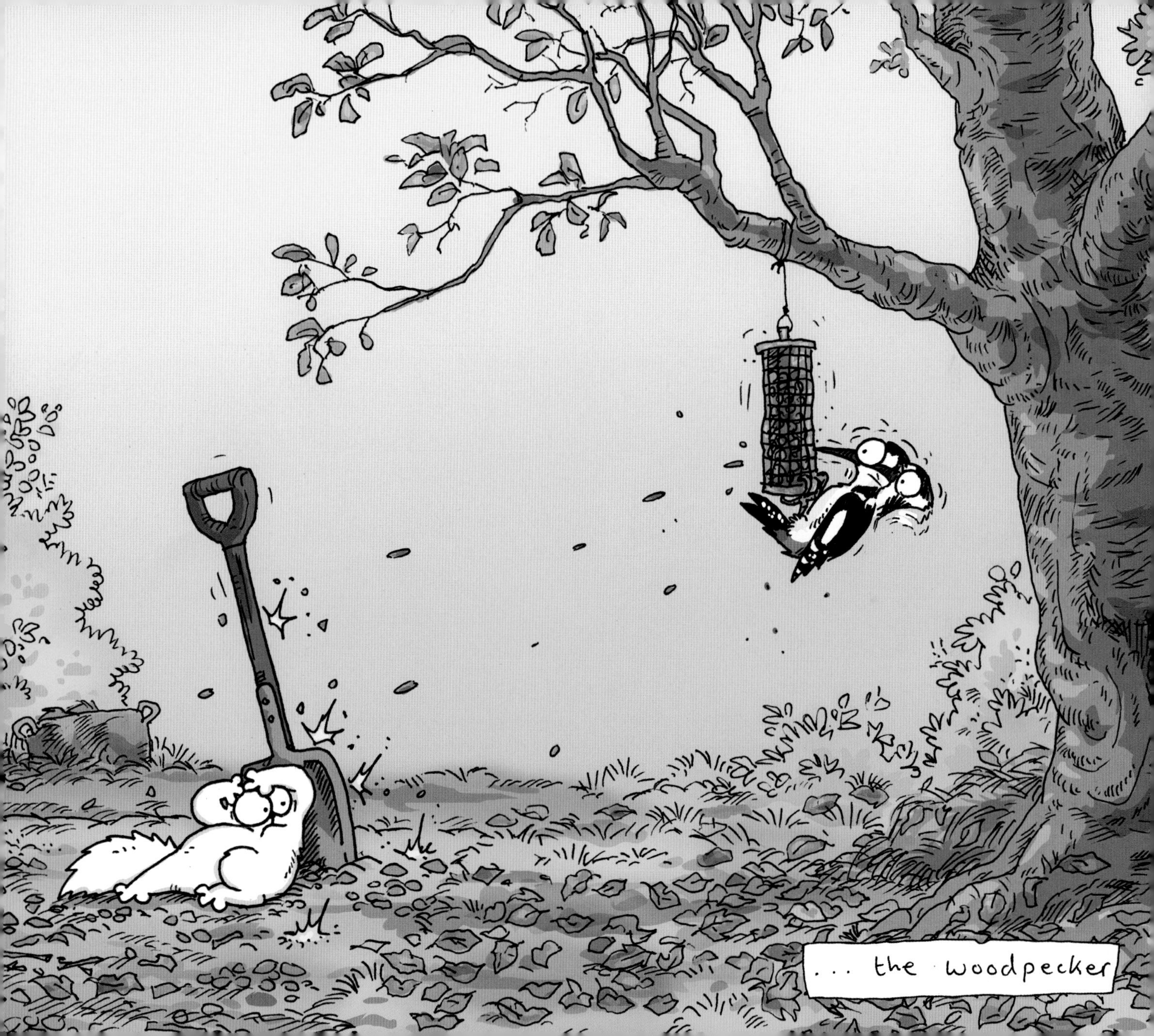
. . . the woodpecker

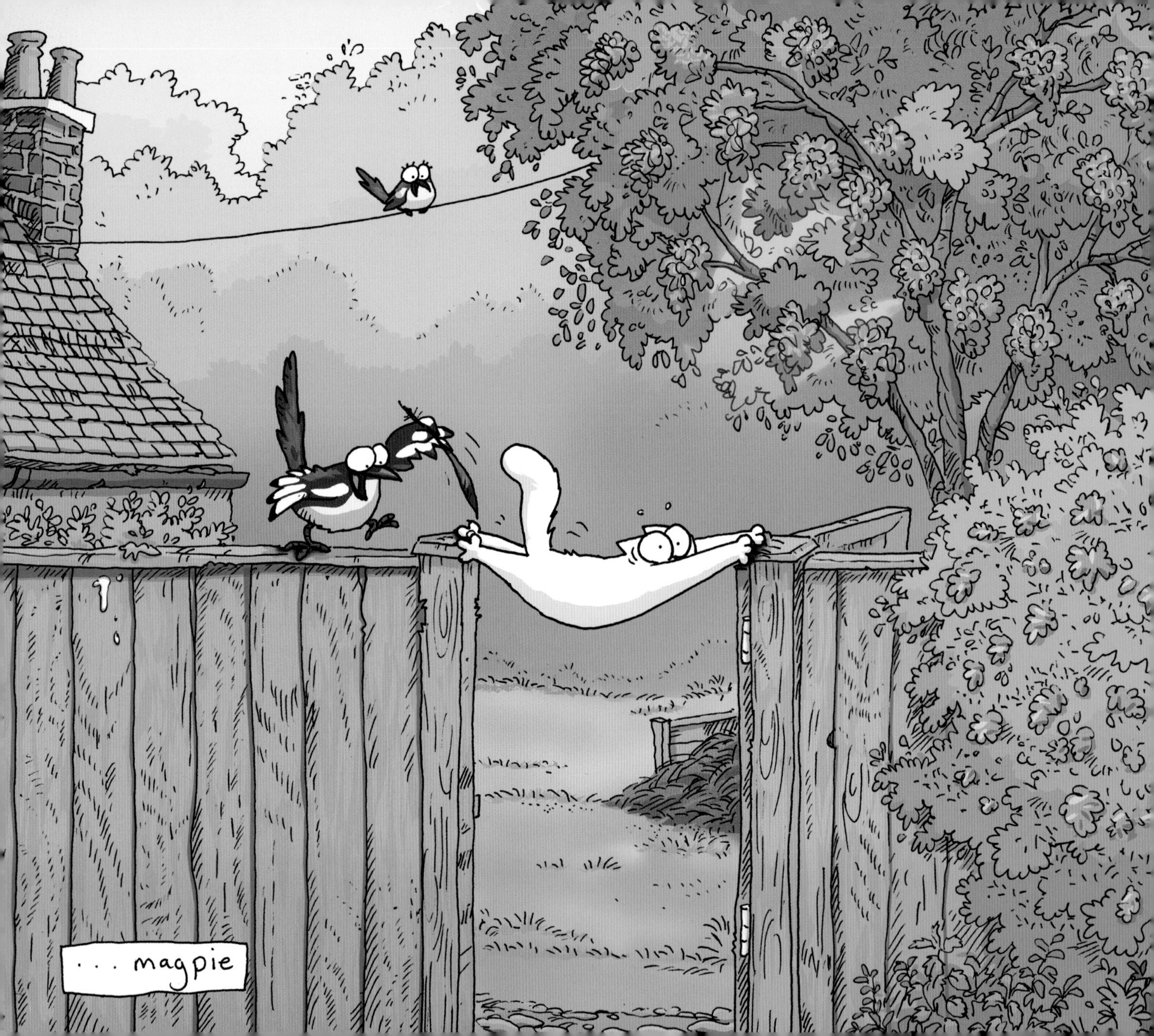
. . . magpie

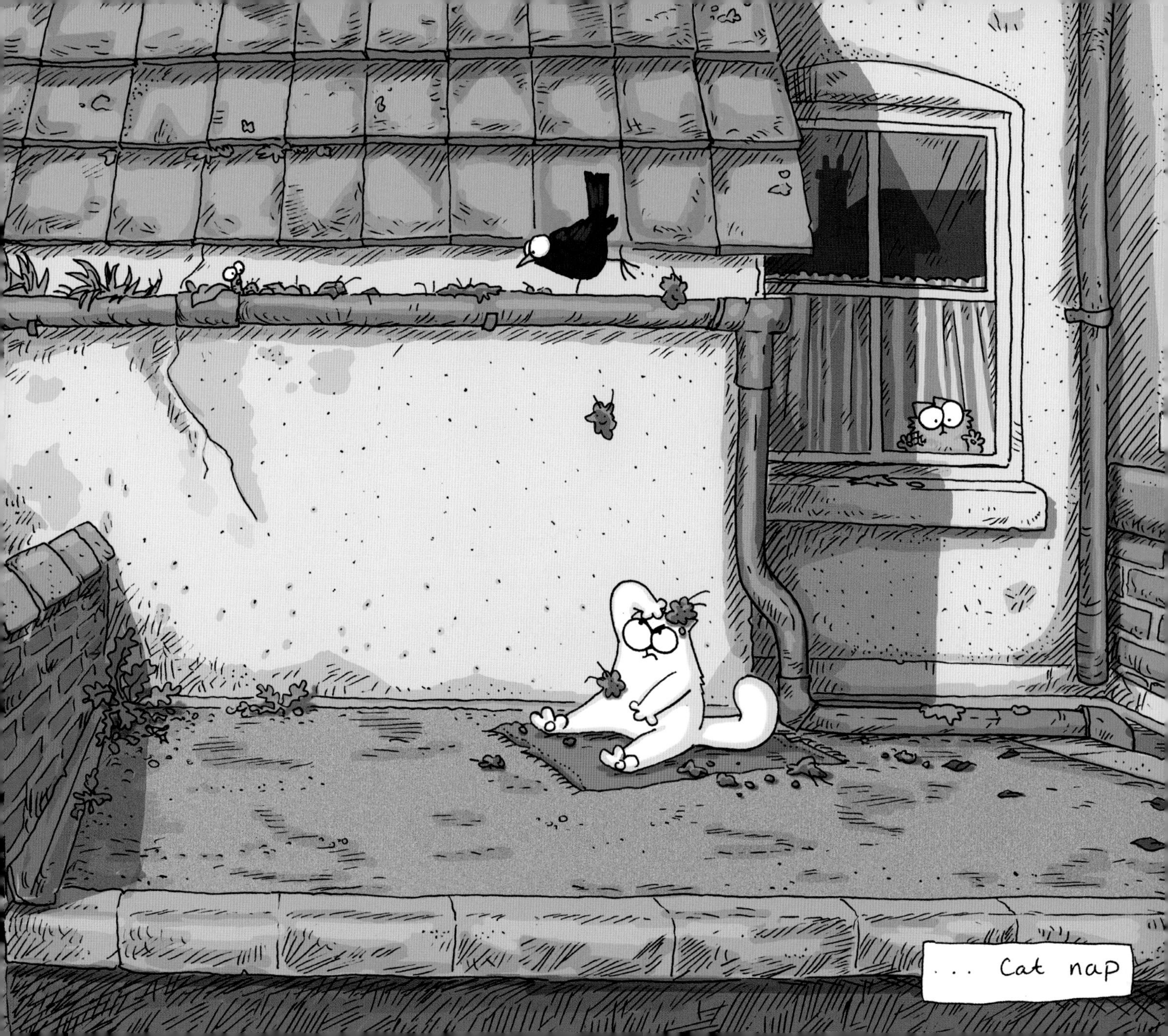
. . . Cat nap

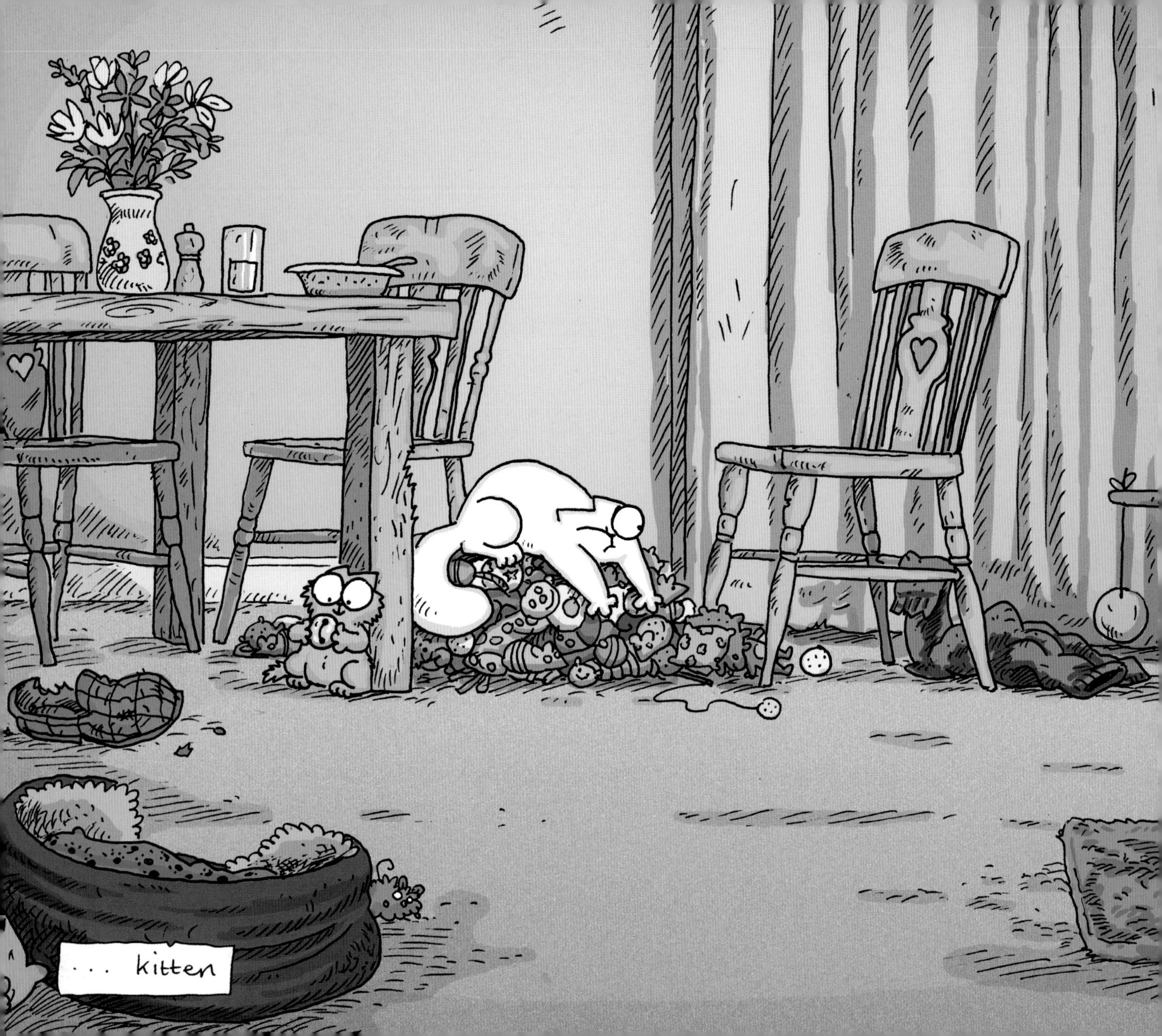
. . . kitten

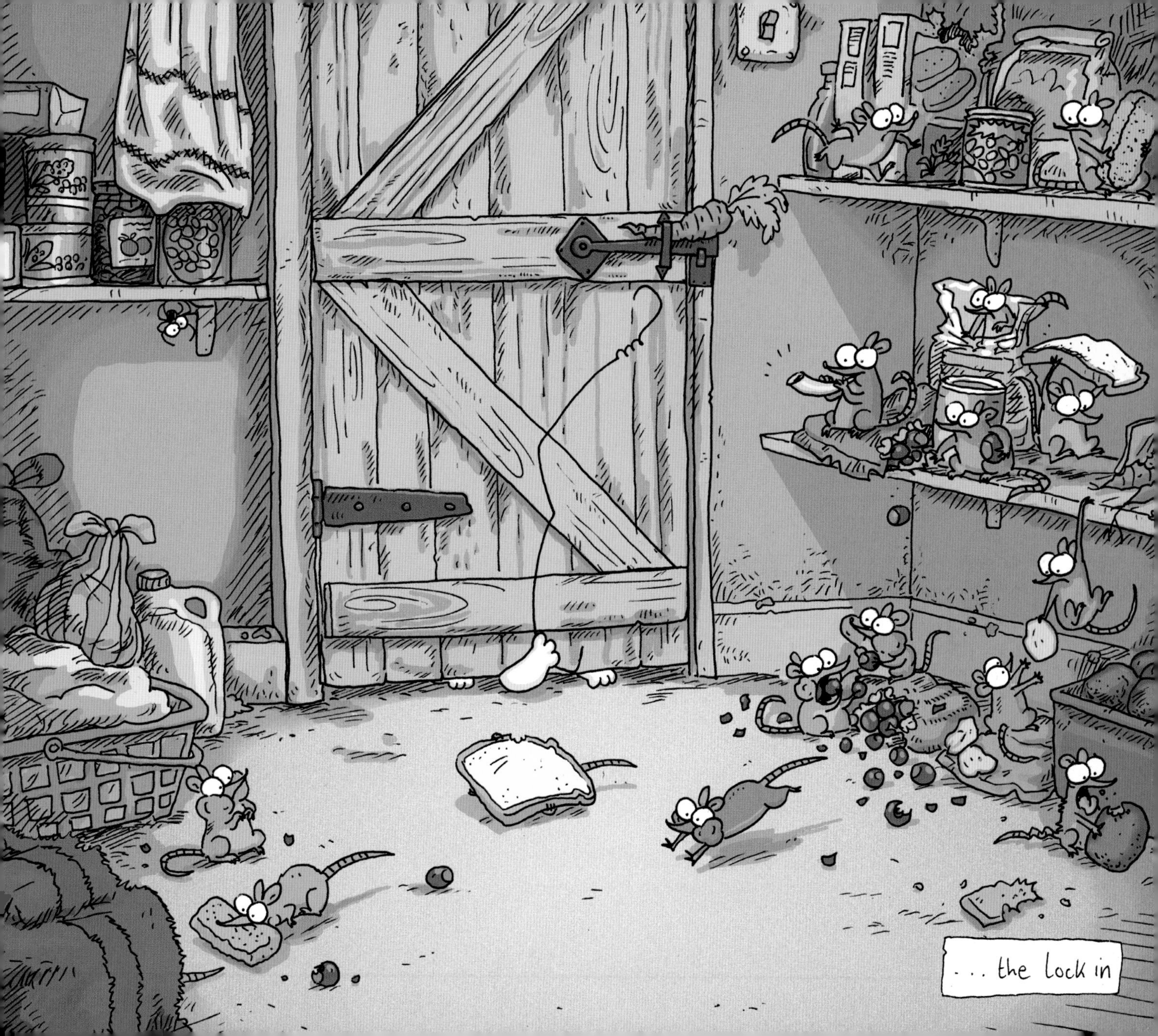
. . . the lock in

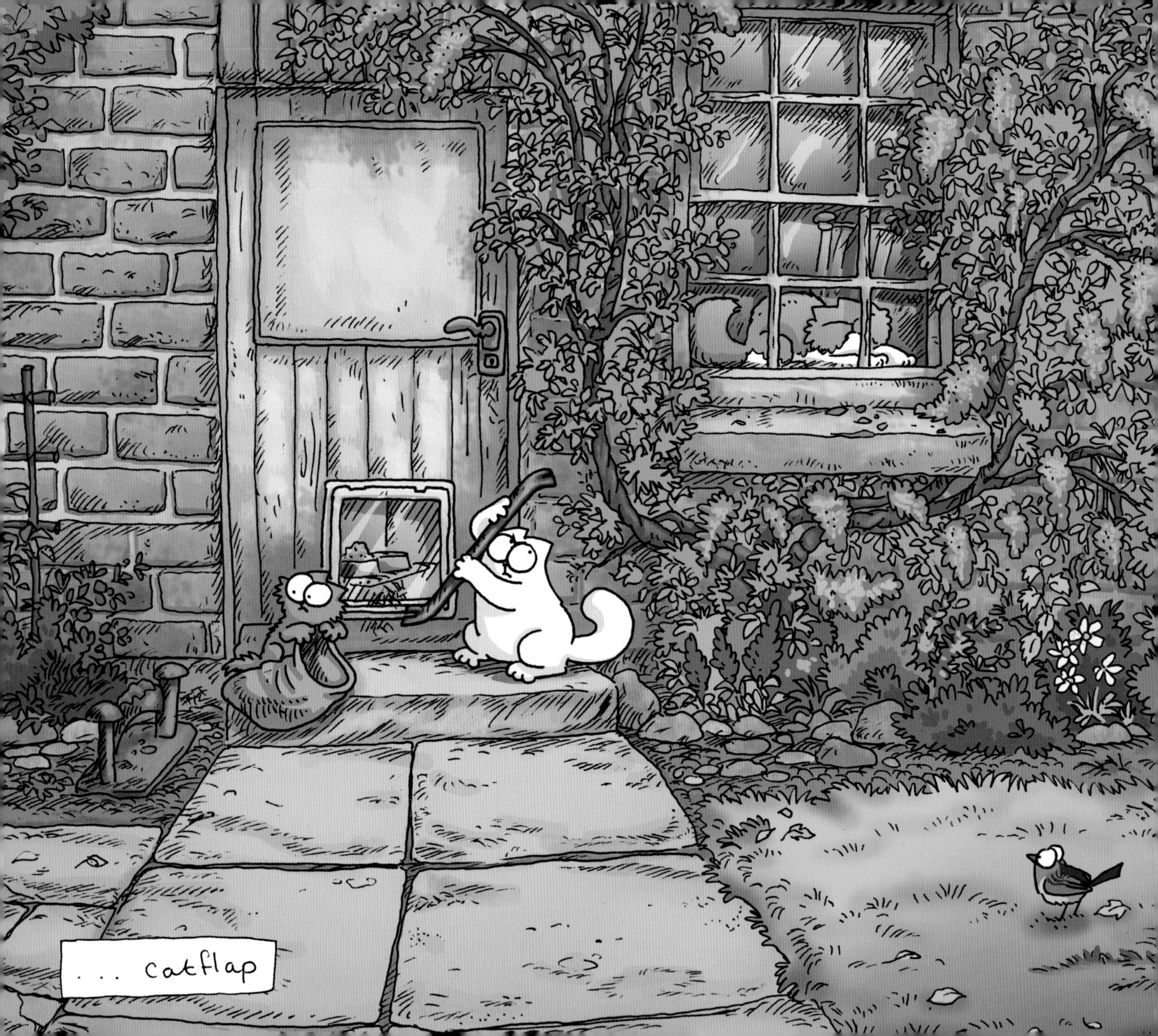
. . . catflap

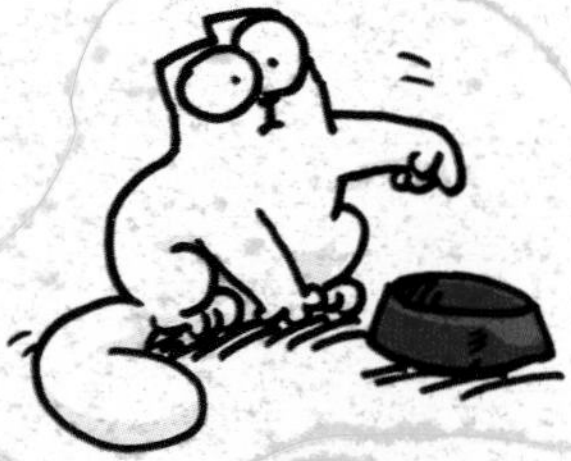

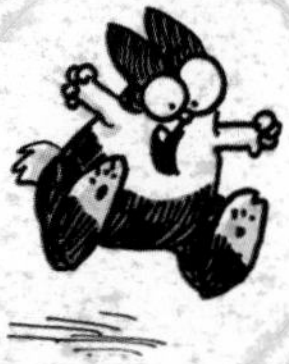

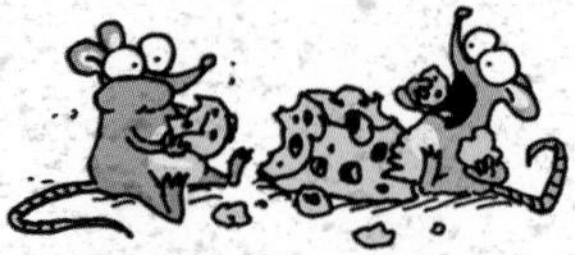

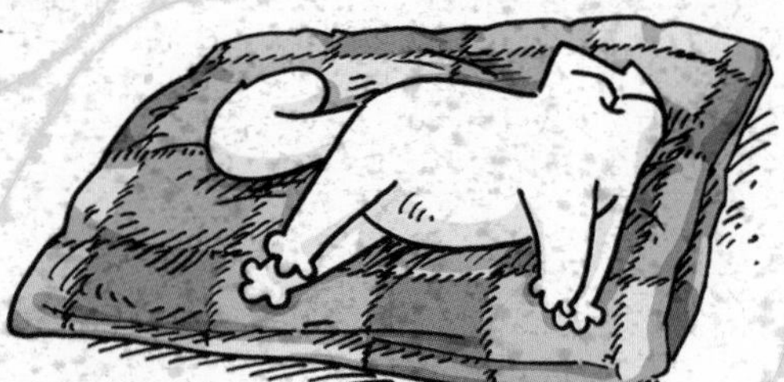

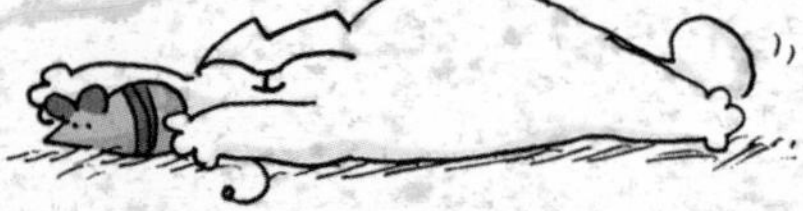

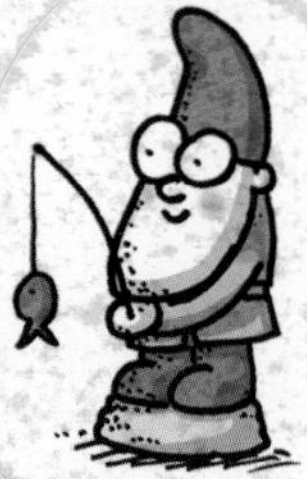

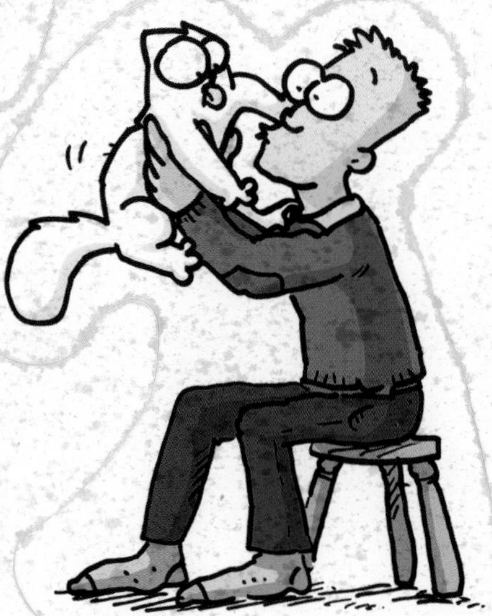

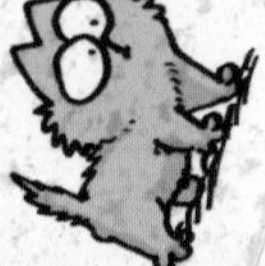

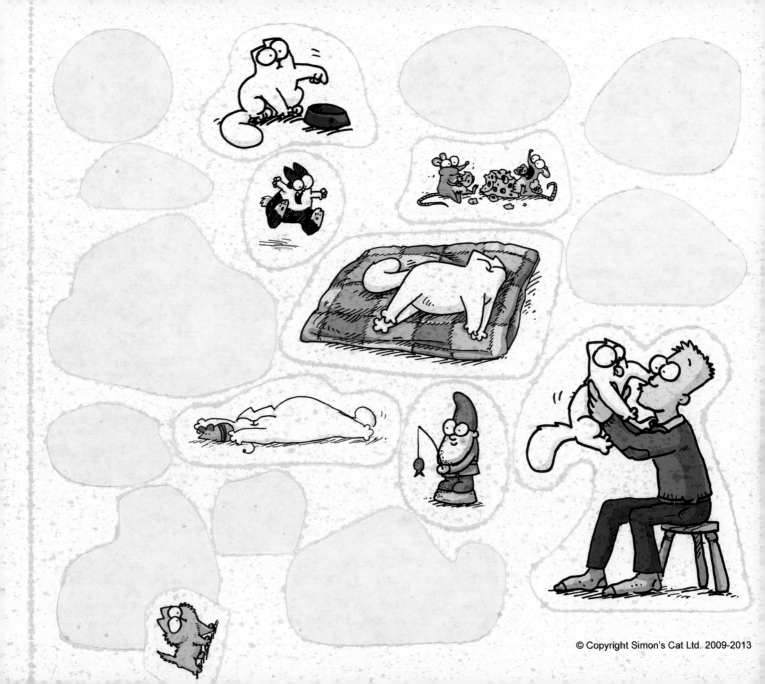

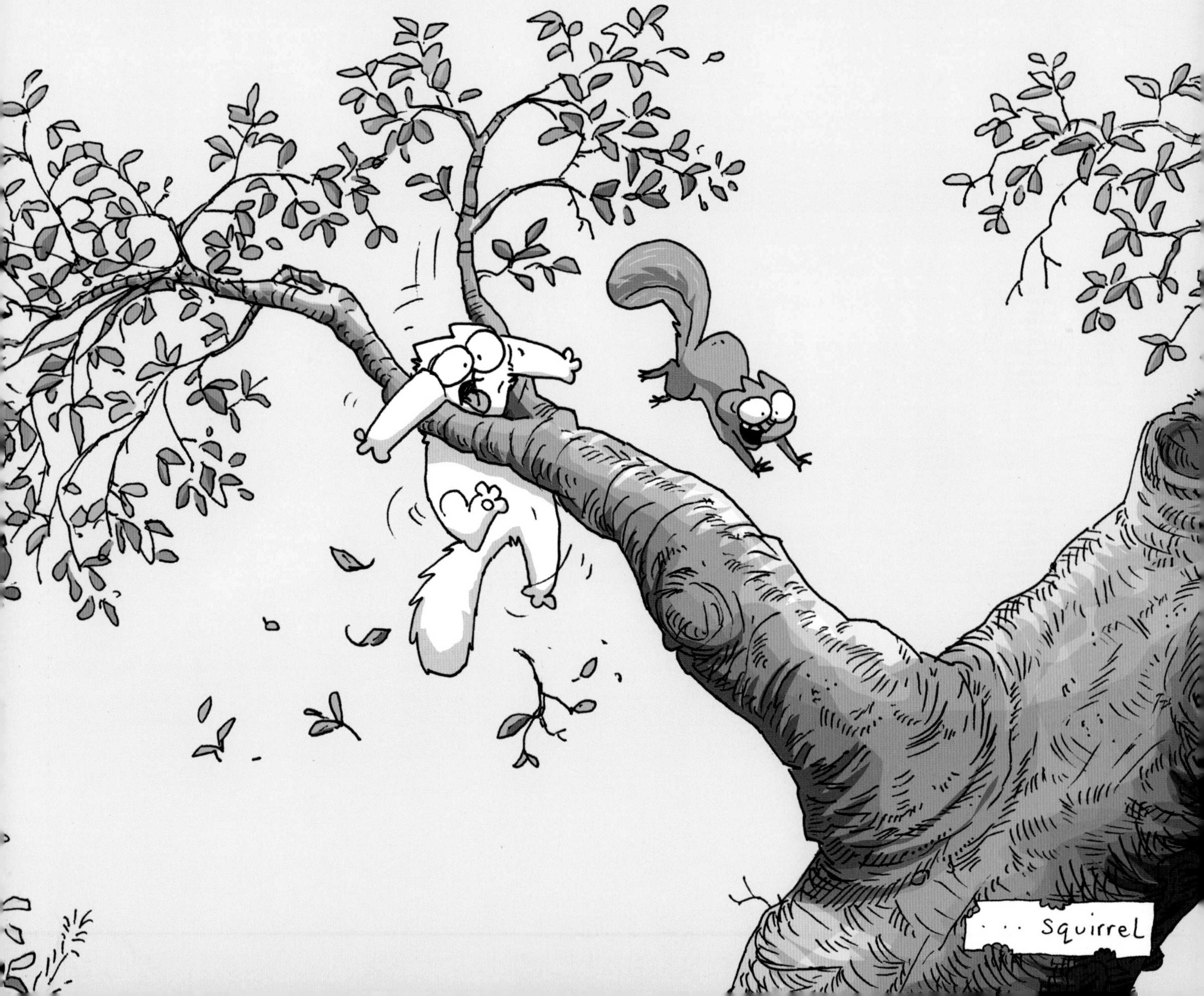
. . . squirreL

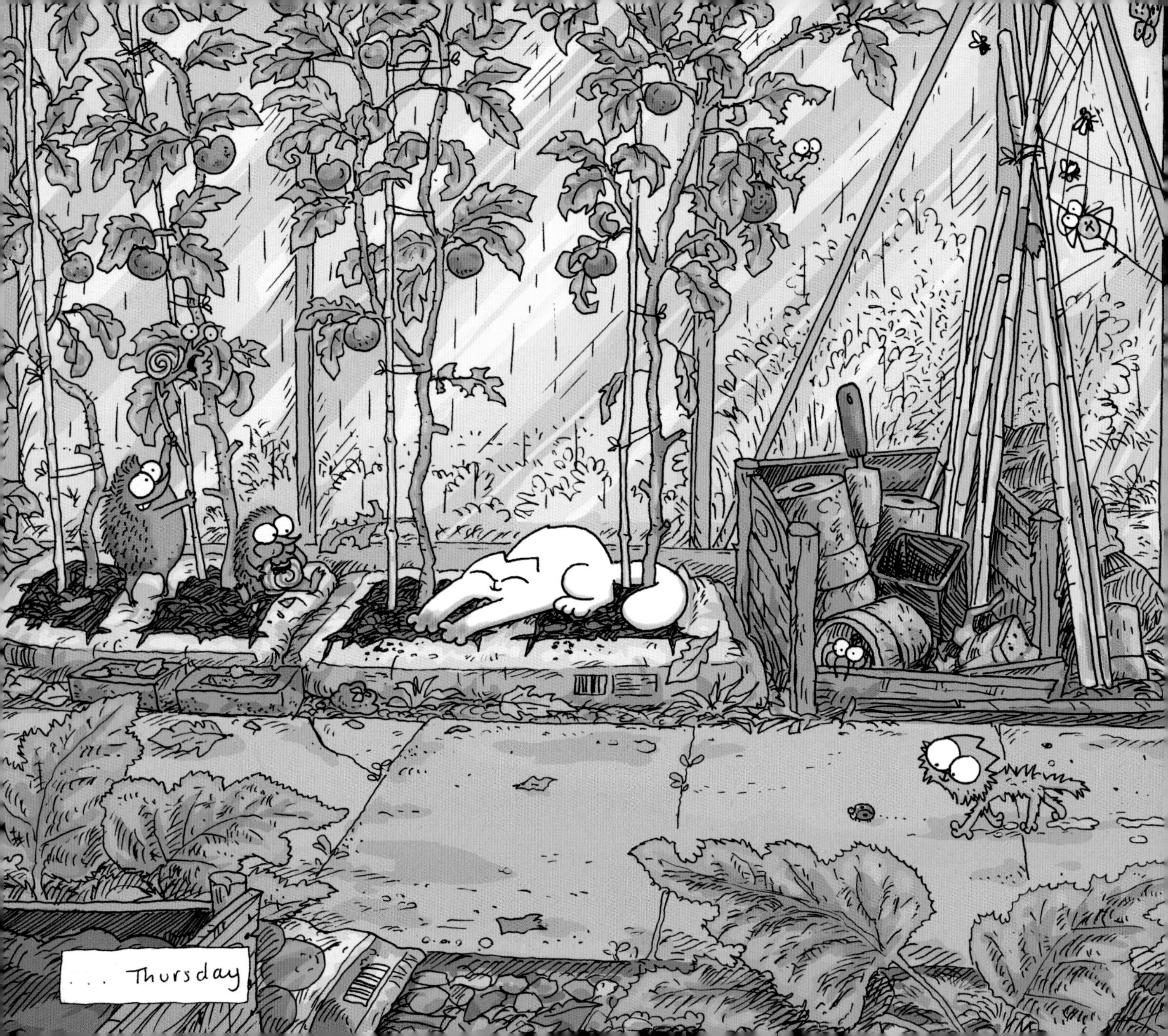
. . . Thursday

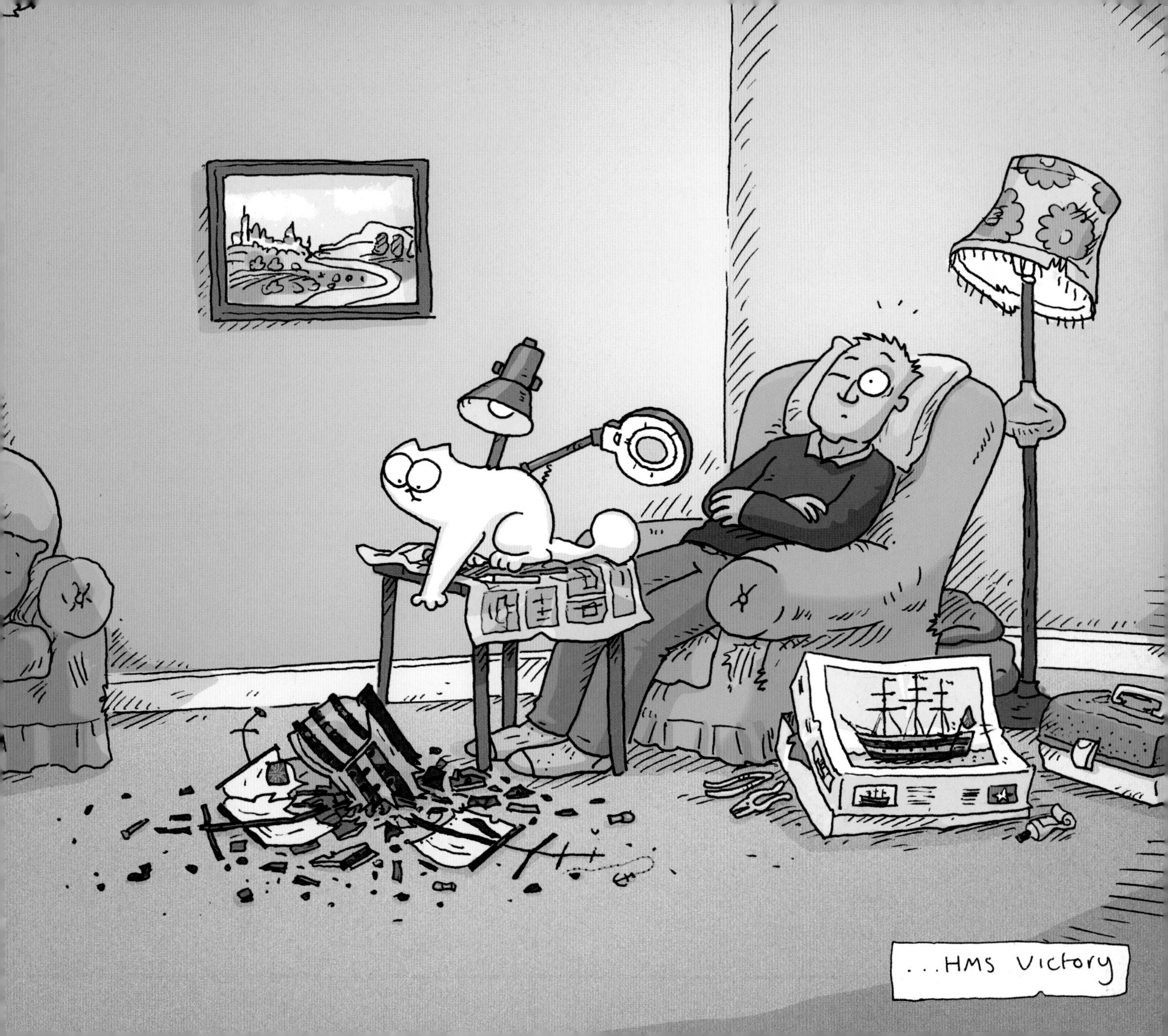

...HMS Victory

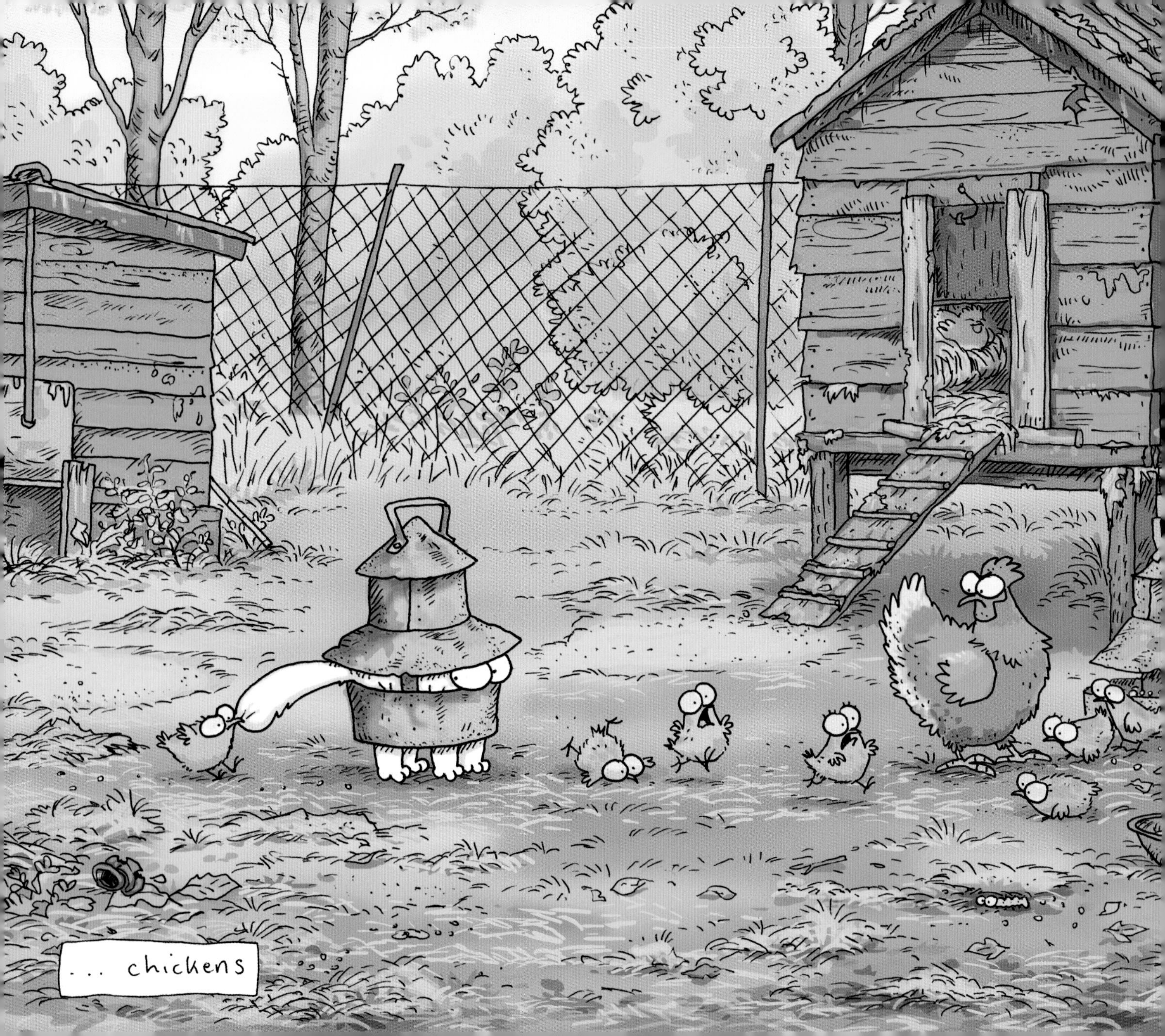
. . . chickens

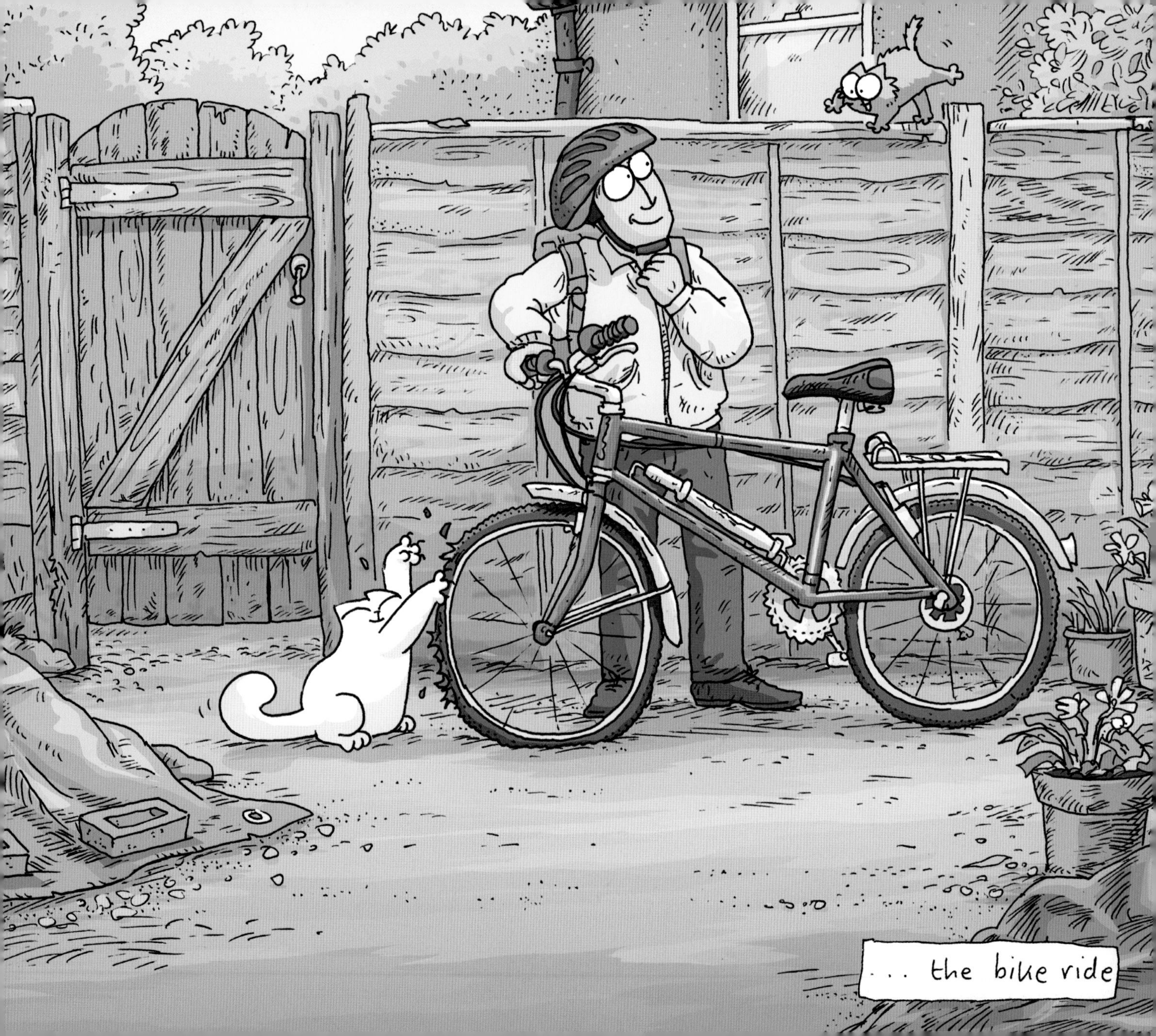
. . . the bike ride

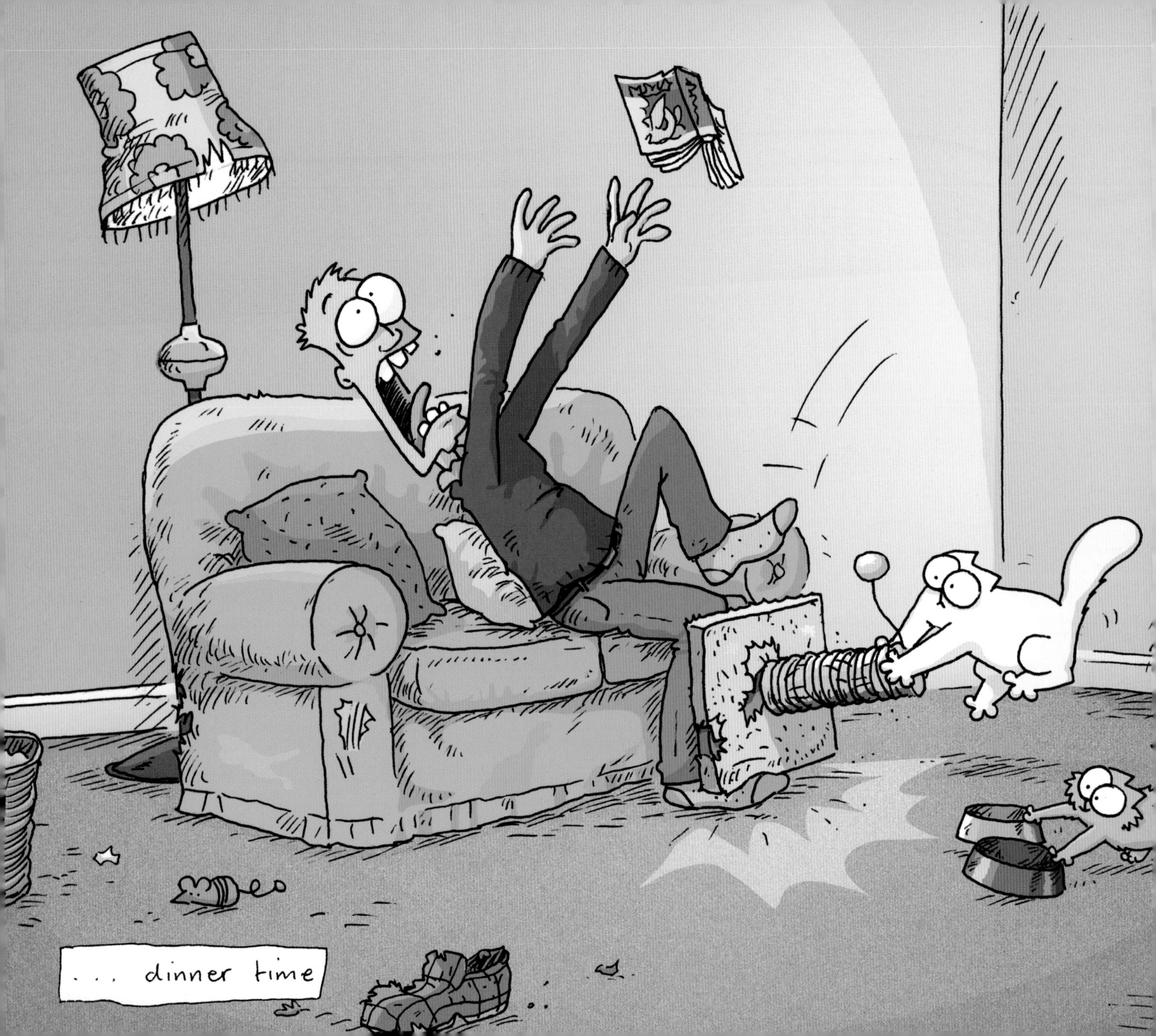
. . . dinner time

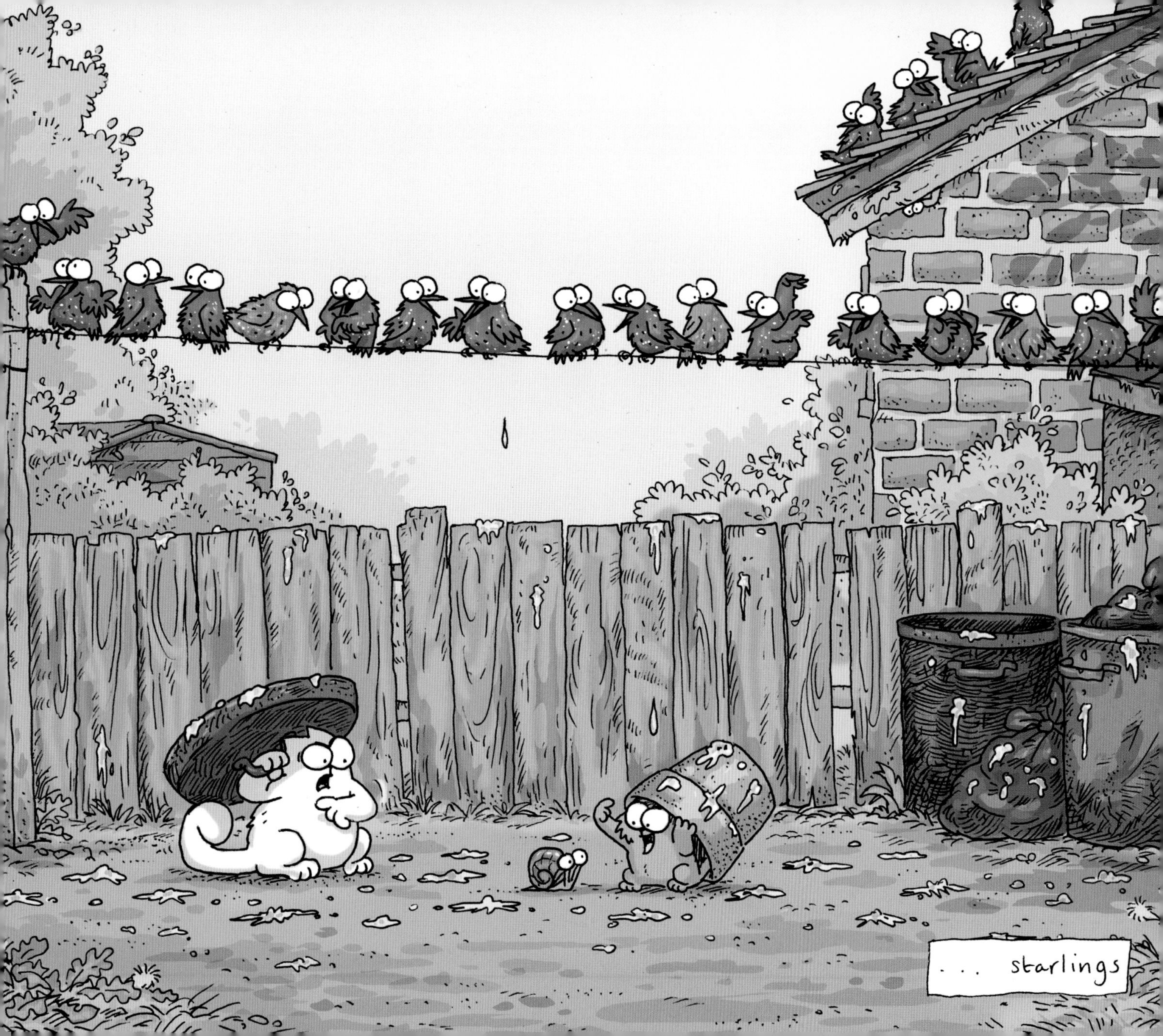
. . . starlings

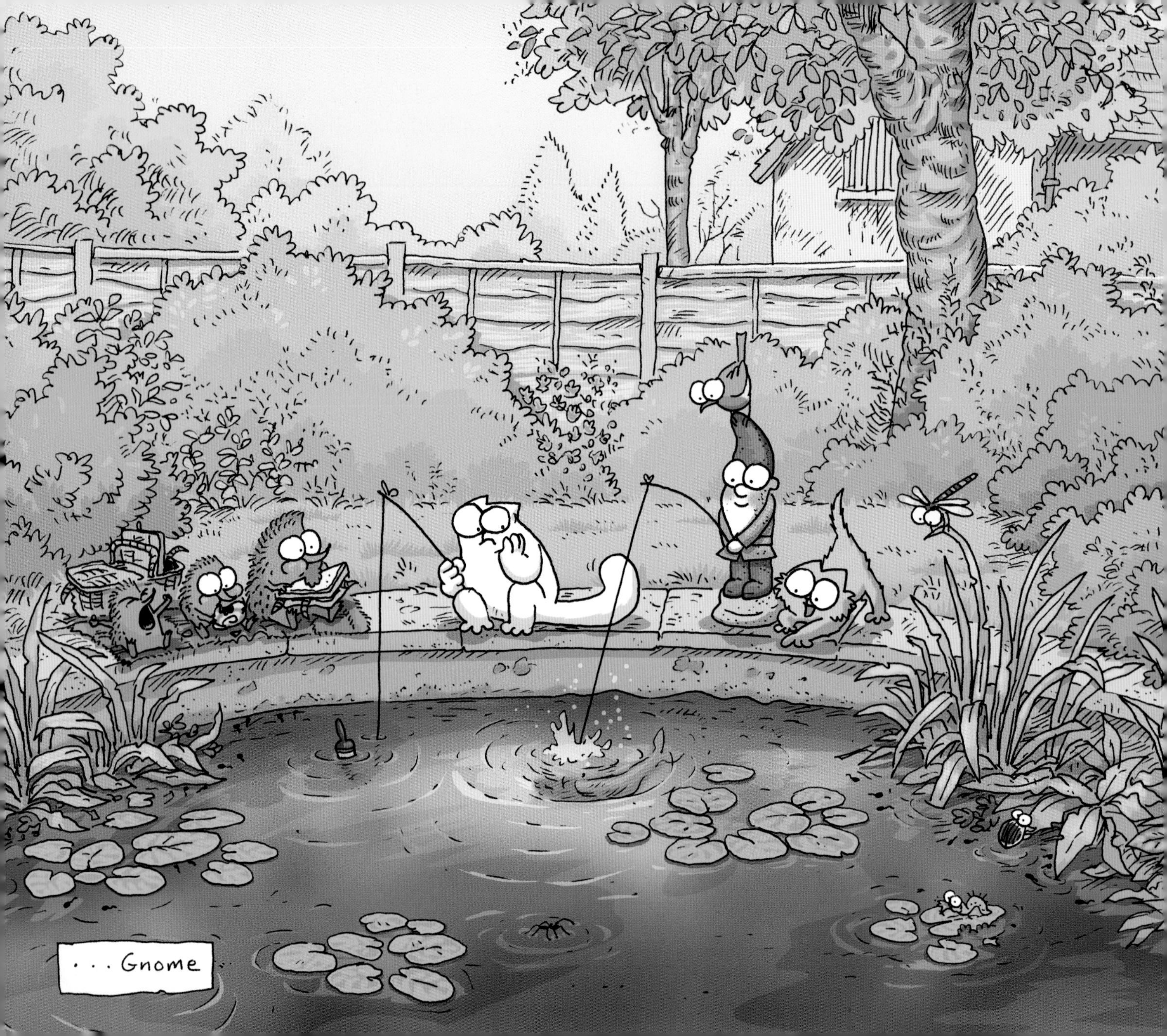
. . . Gnome

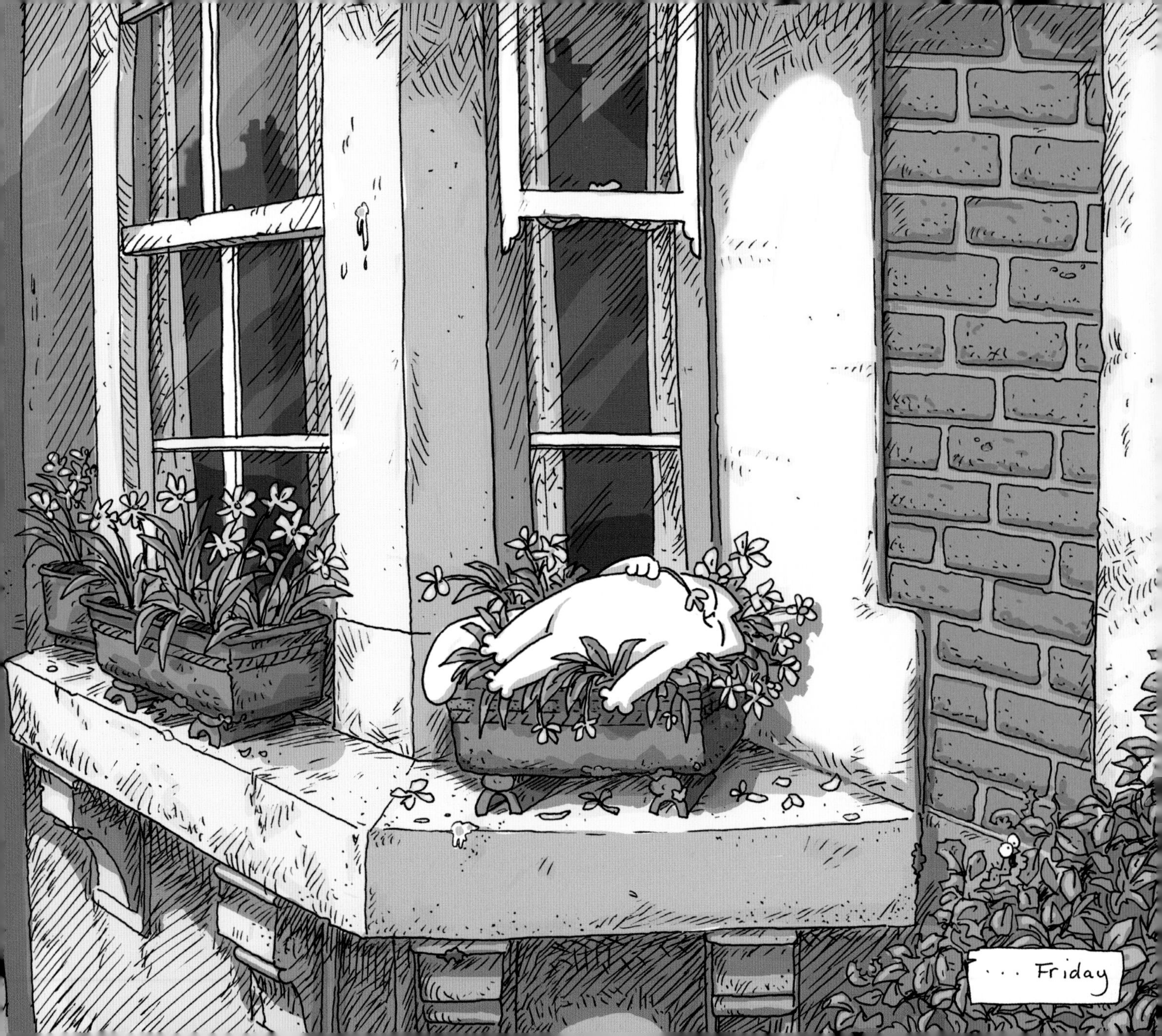
. . . Friday

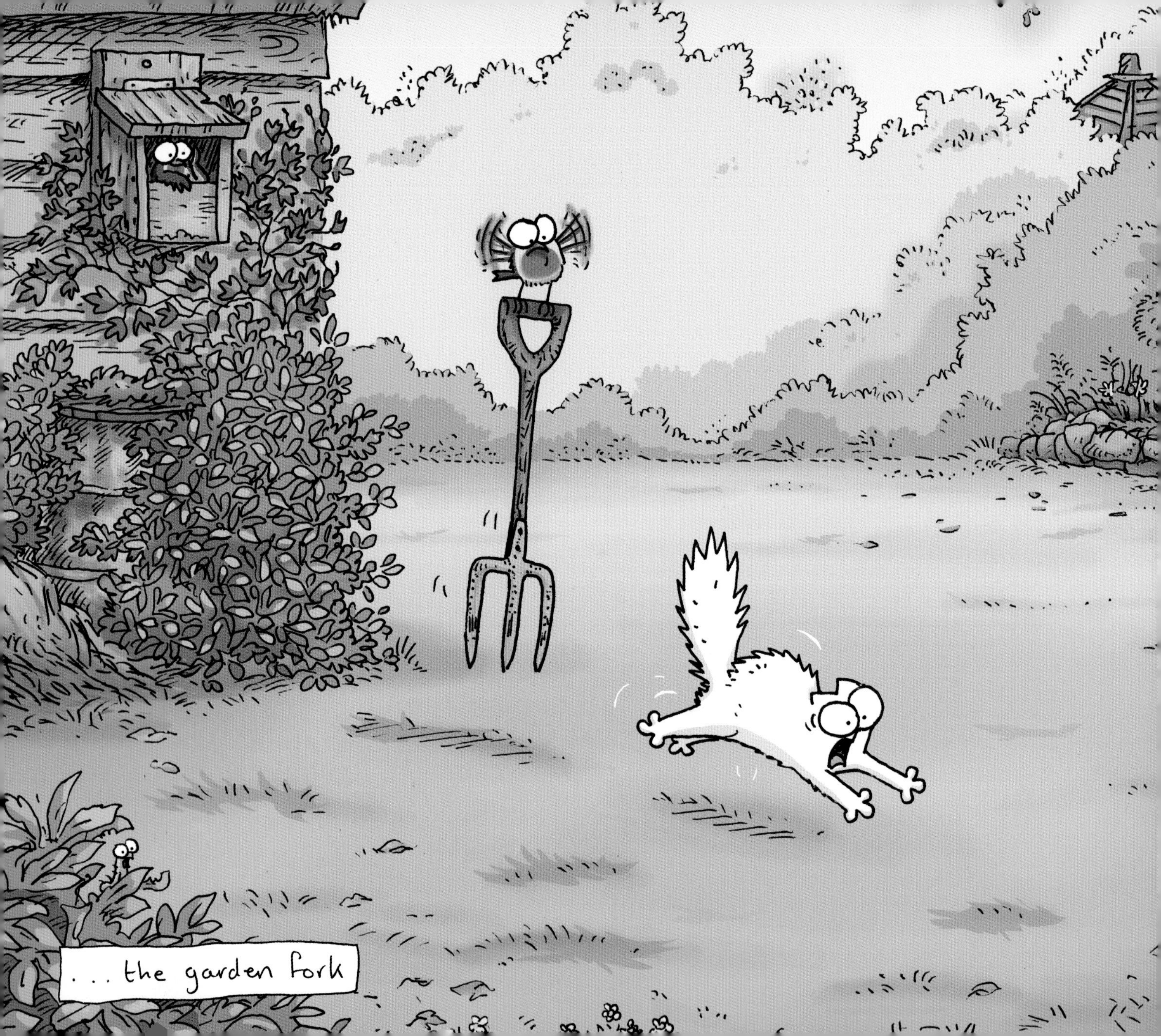
. . . the garden fork

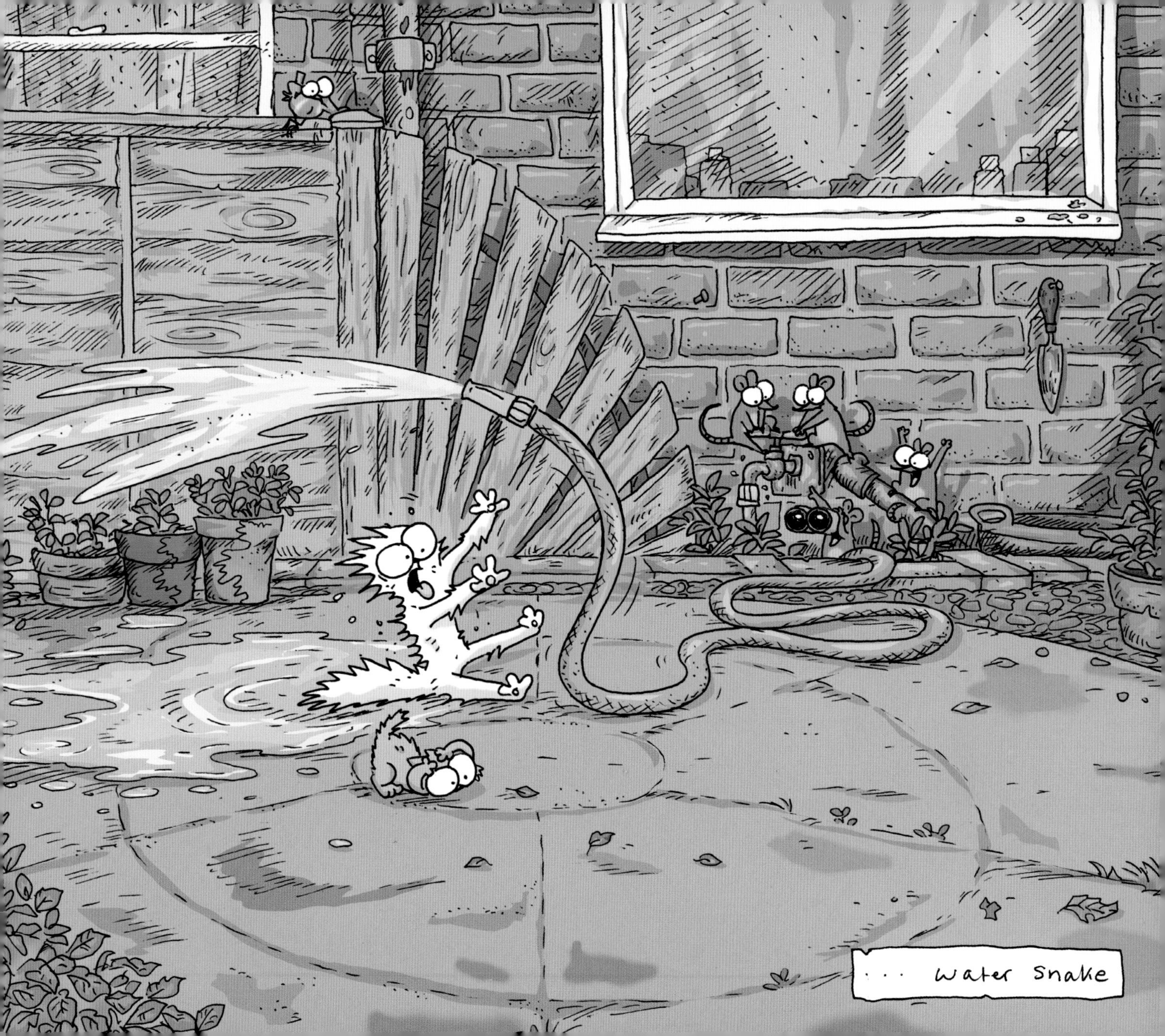
. . . Water Snake

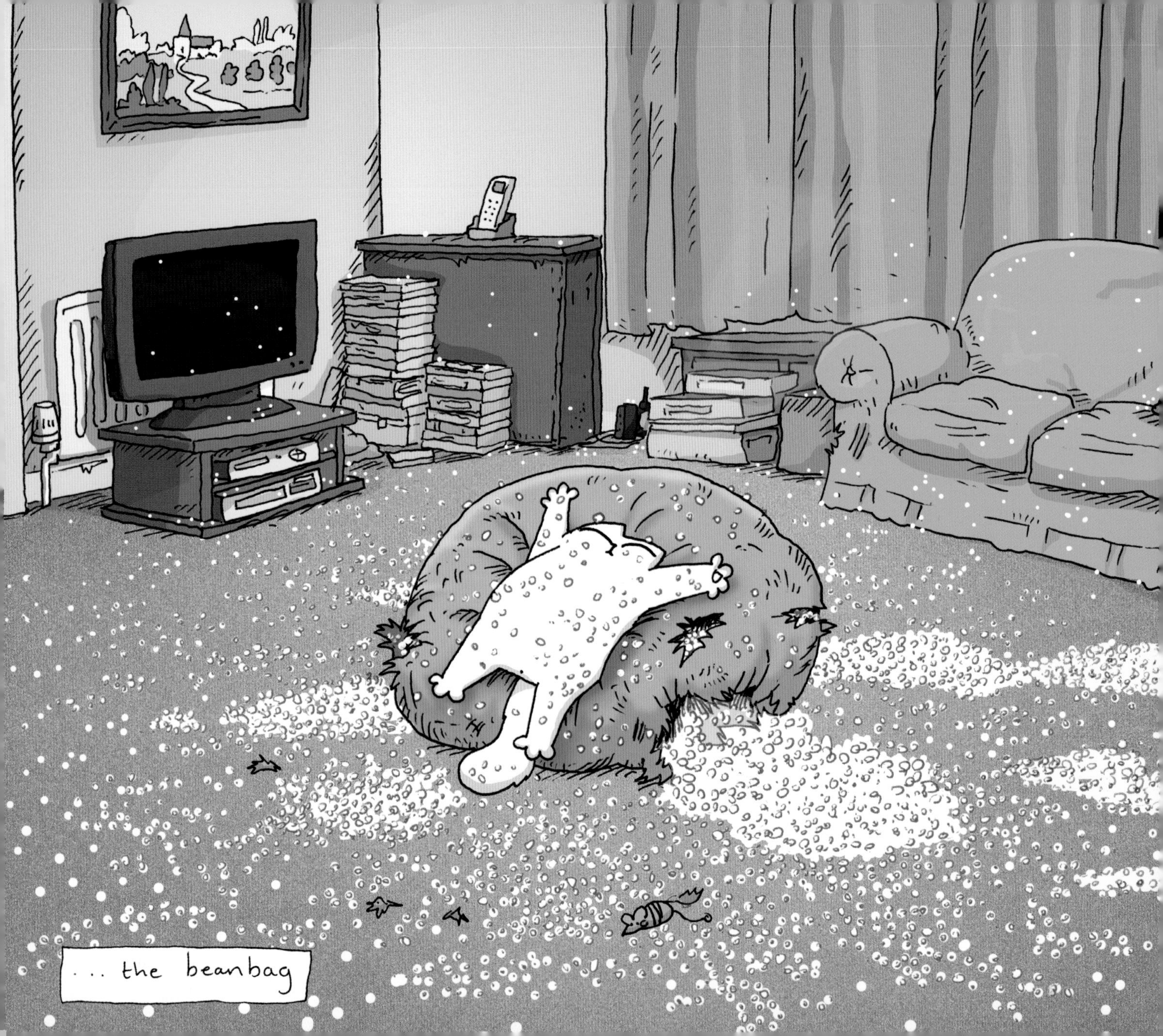
. . . the beanbag

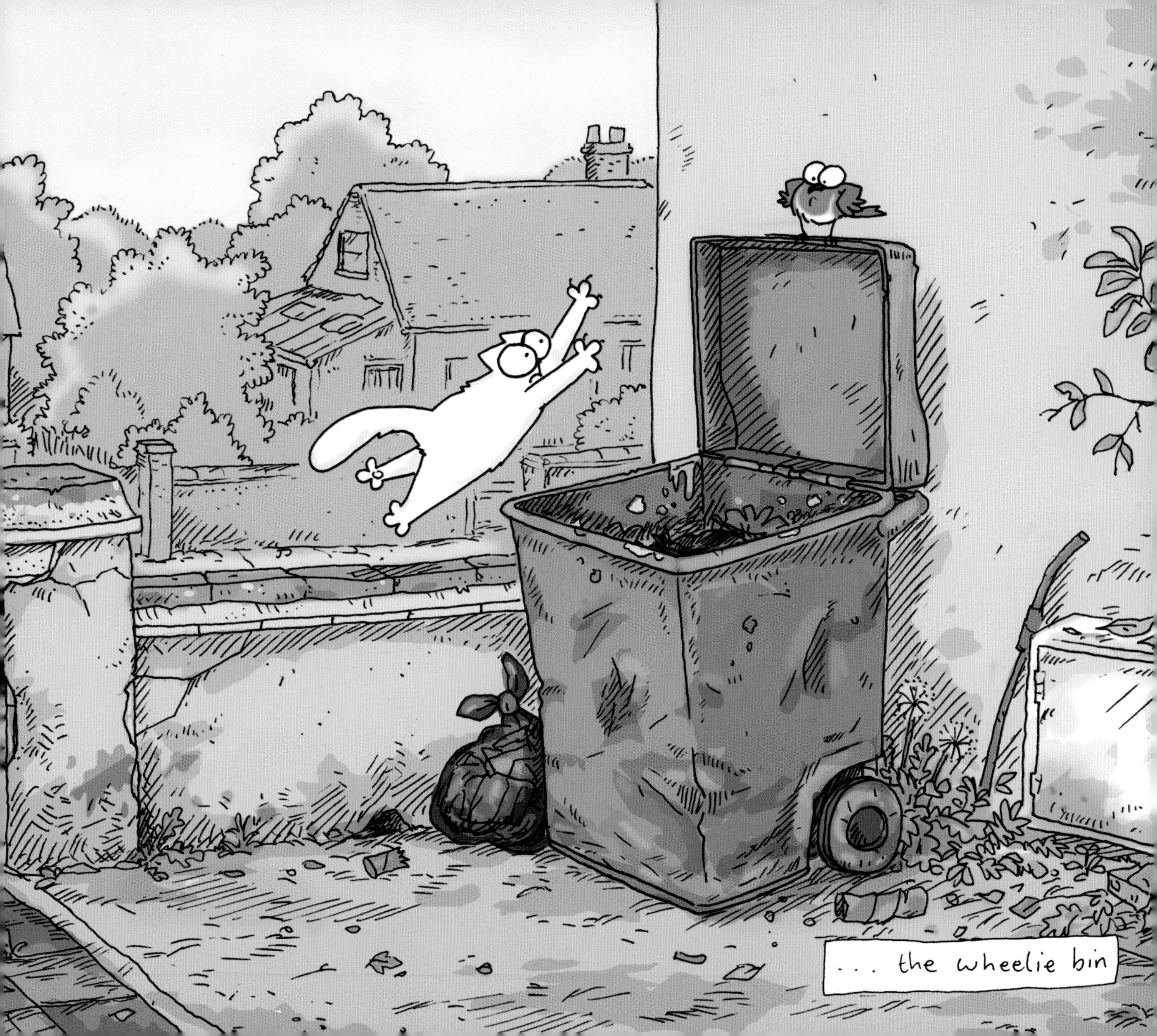
. . . the wheelie bin

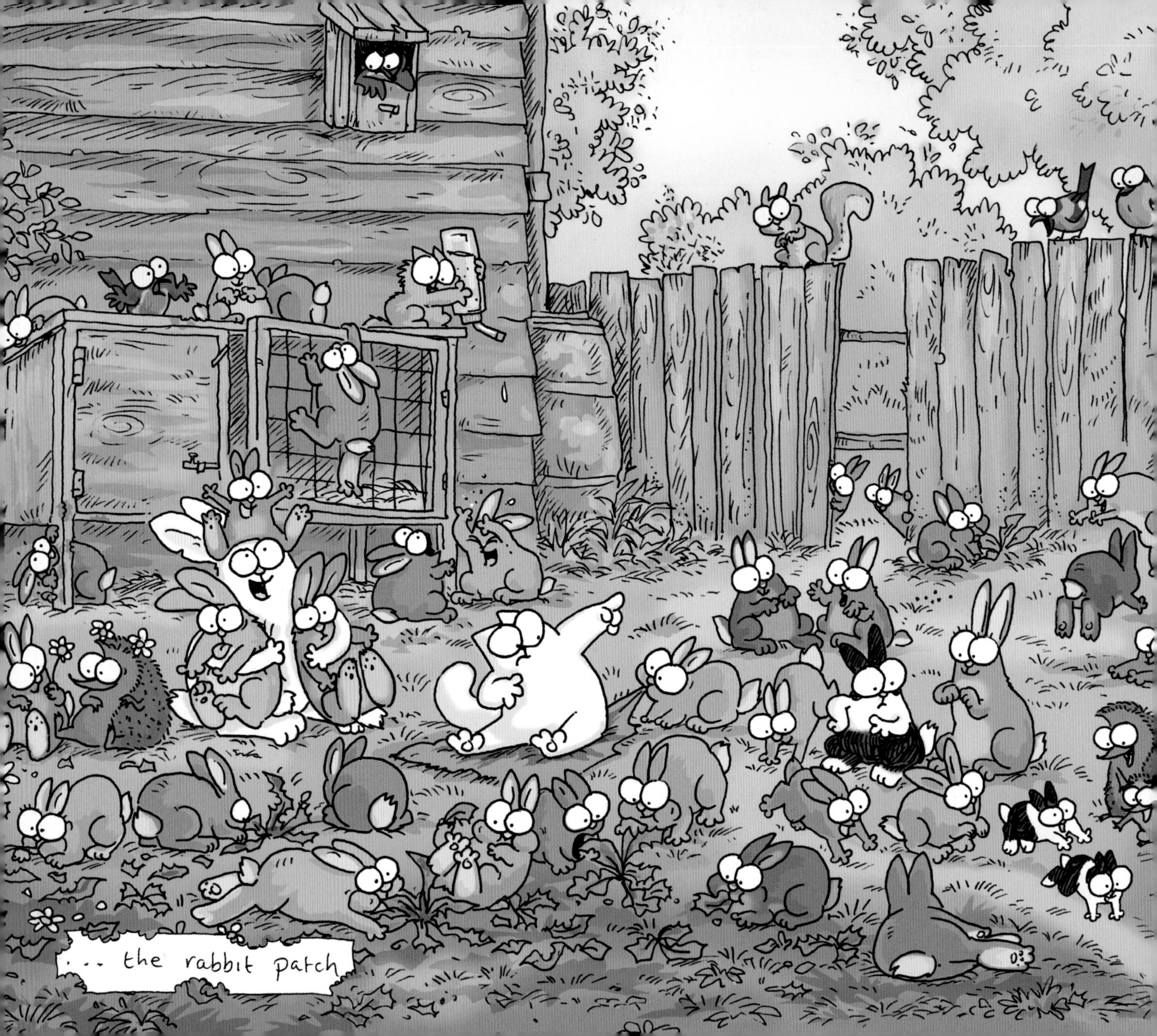
... the rabbit patch

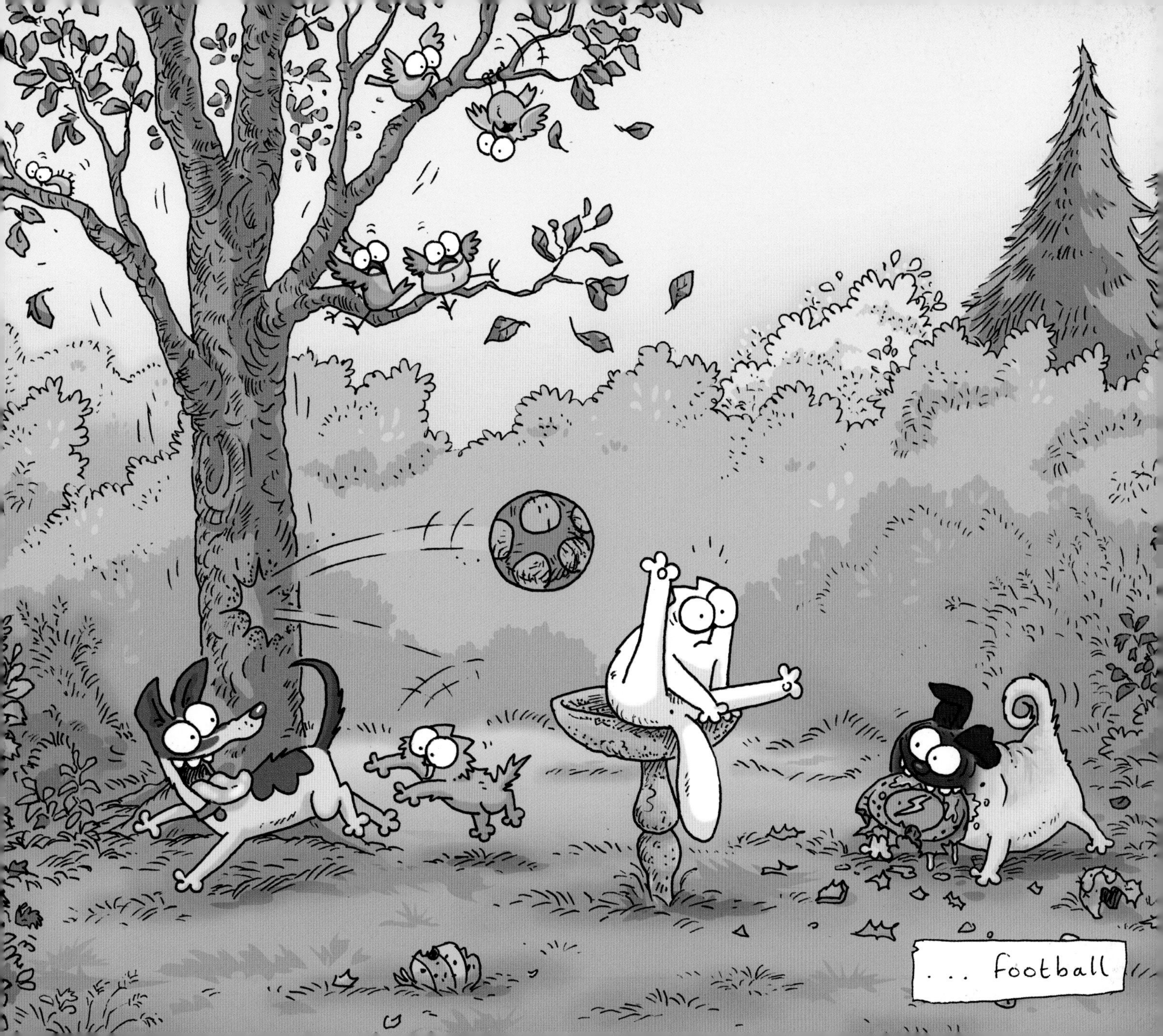
. . . football

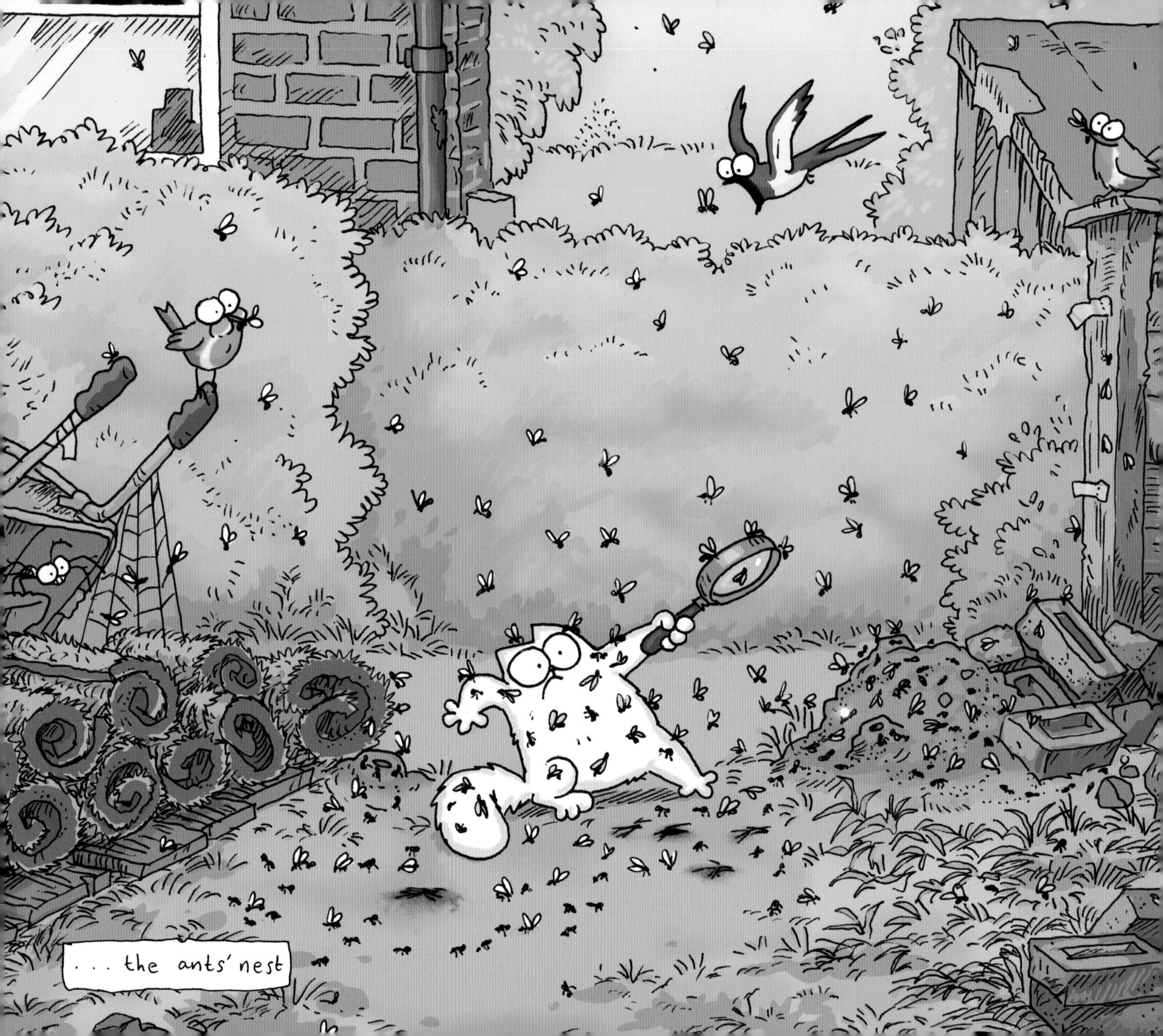
. . . the ants' nest

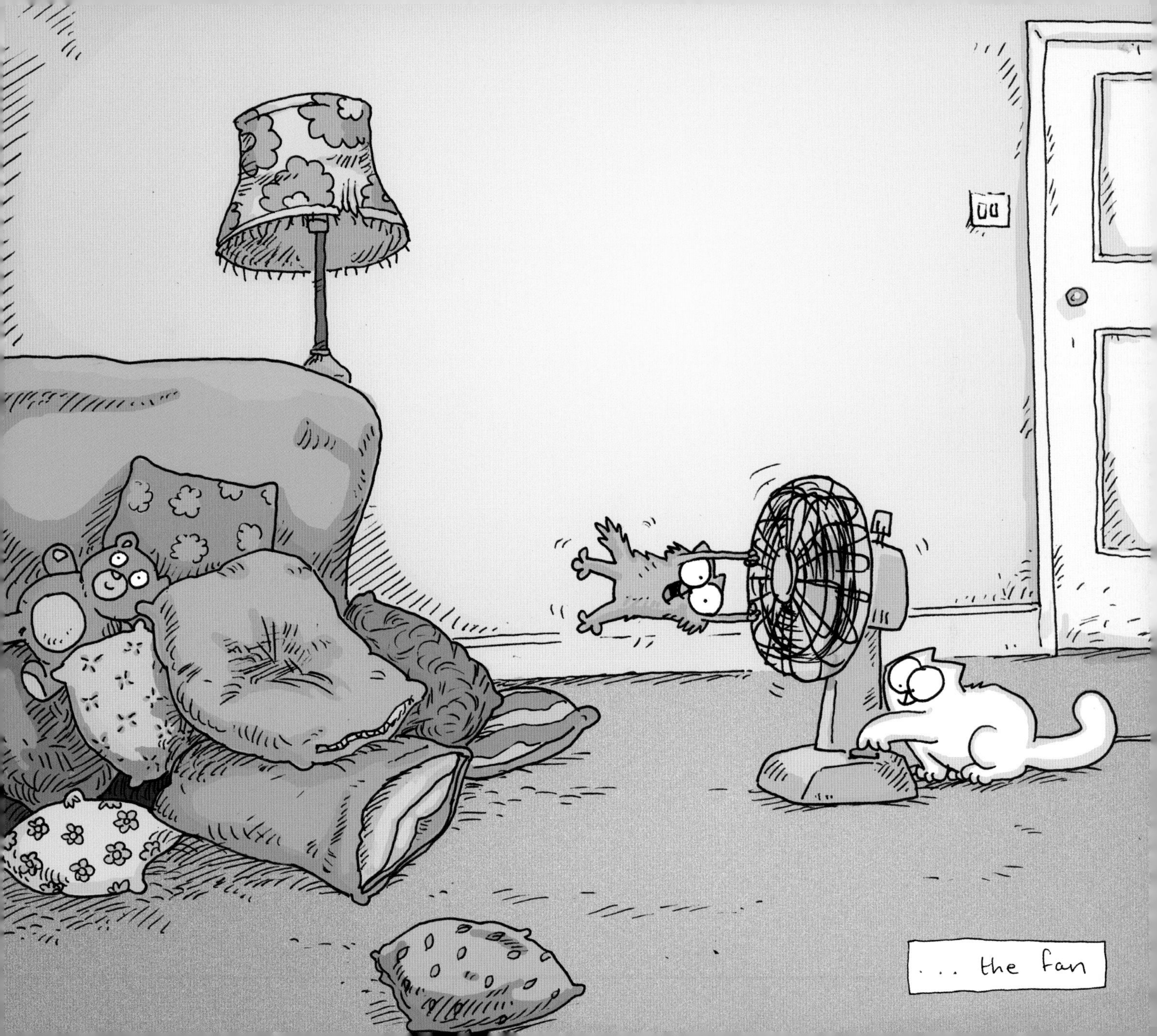
. . . the fan

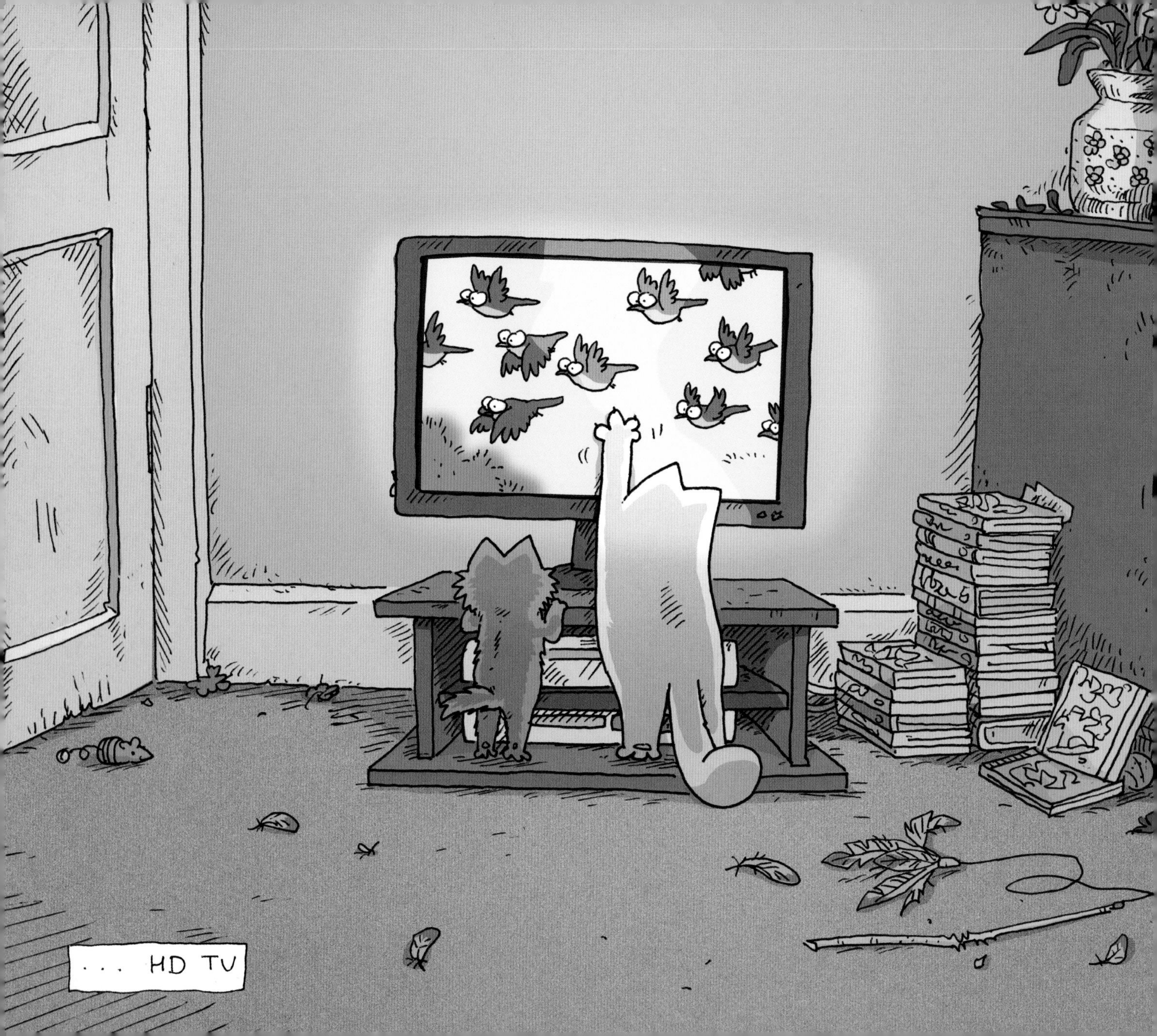
. . . HD TV

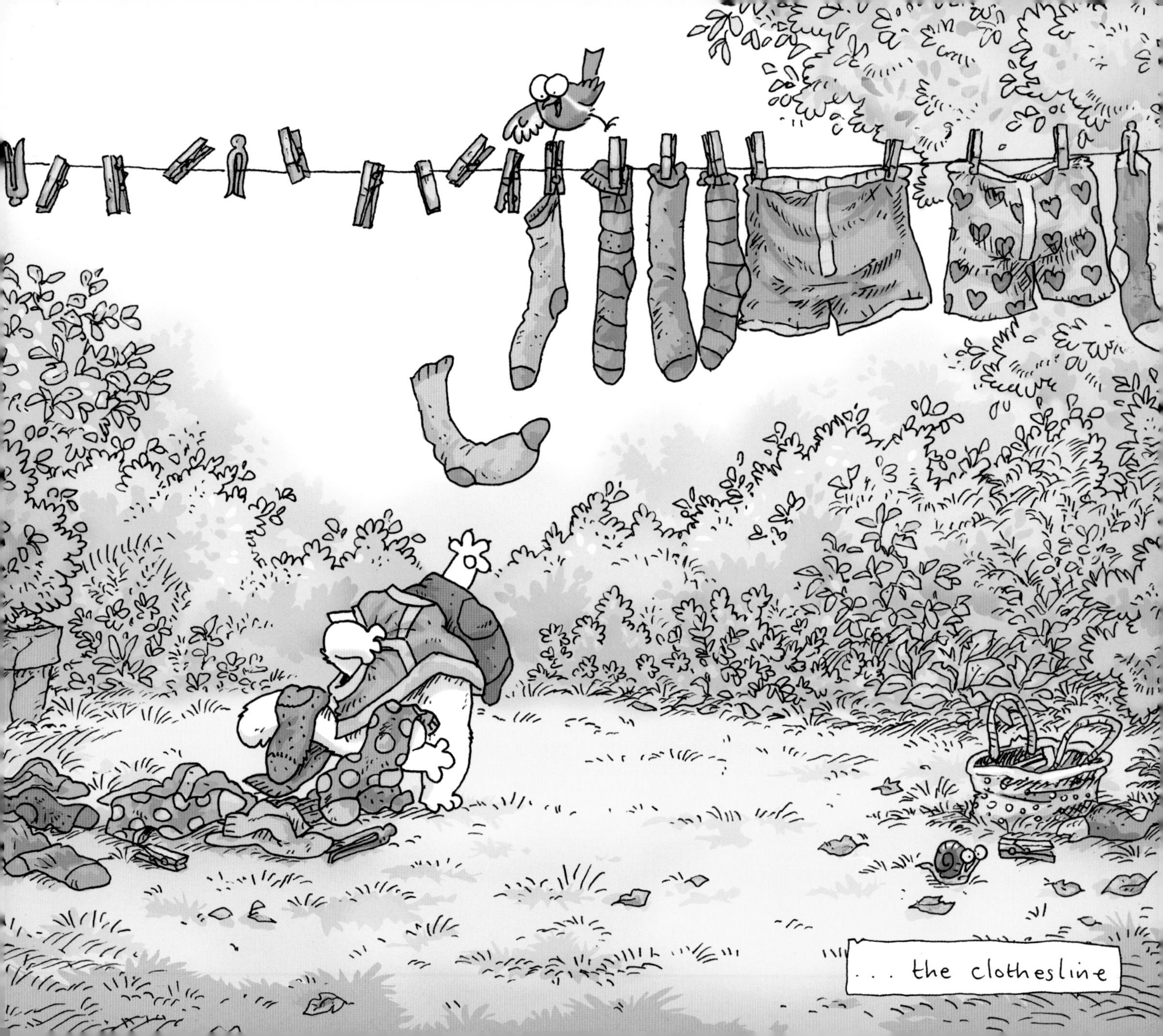
. . . the clothesline

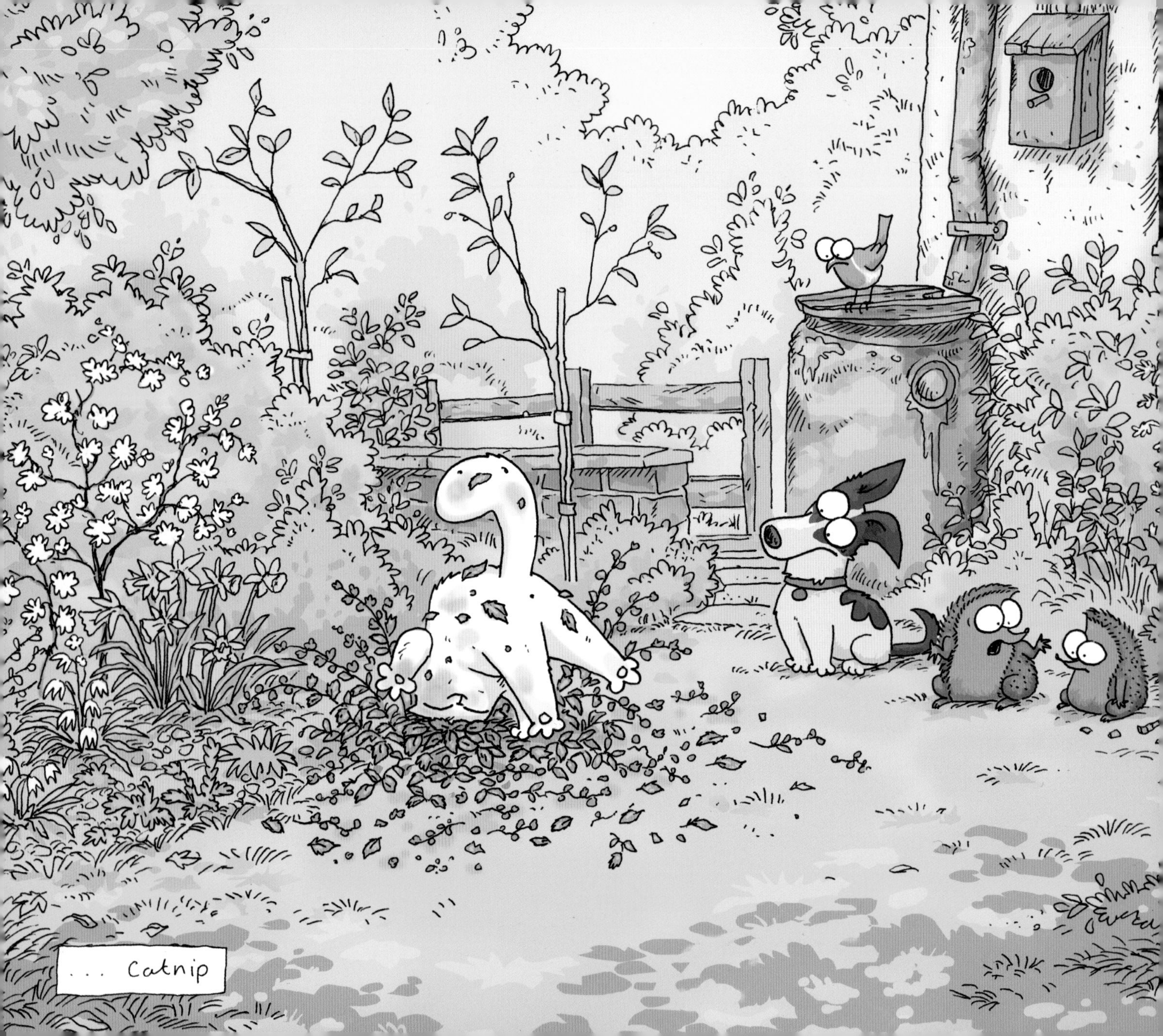
. . . Catnip

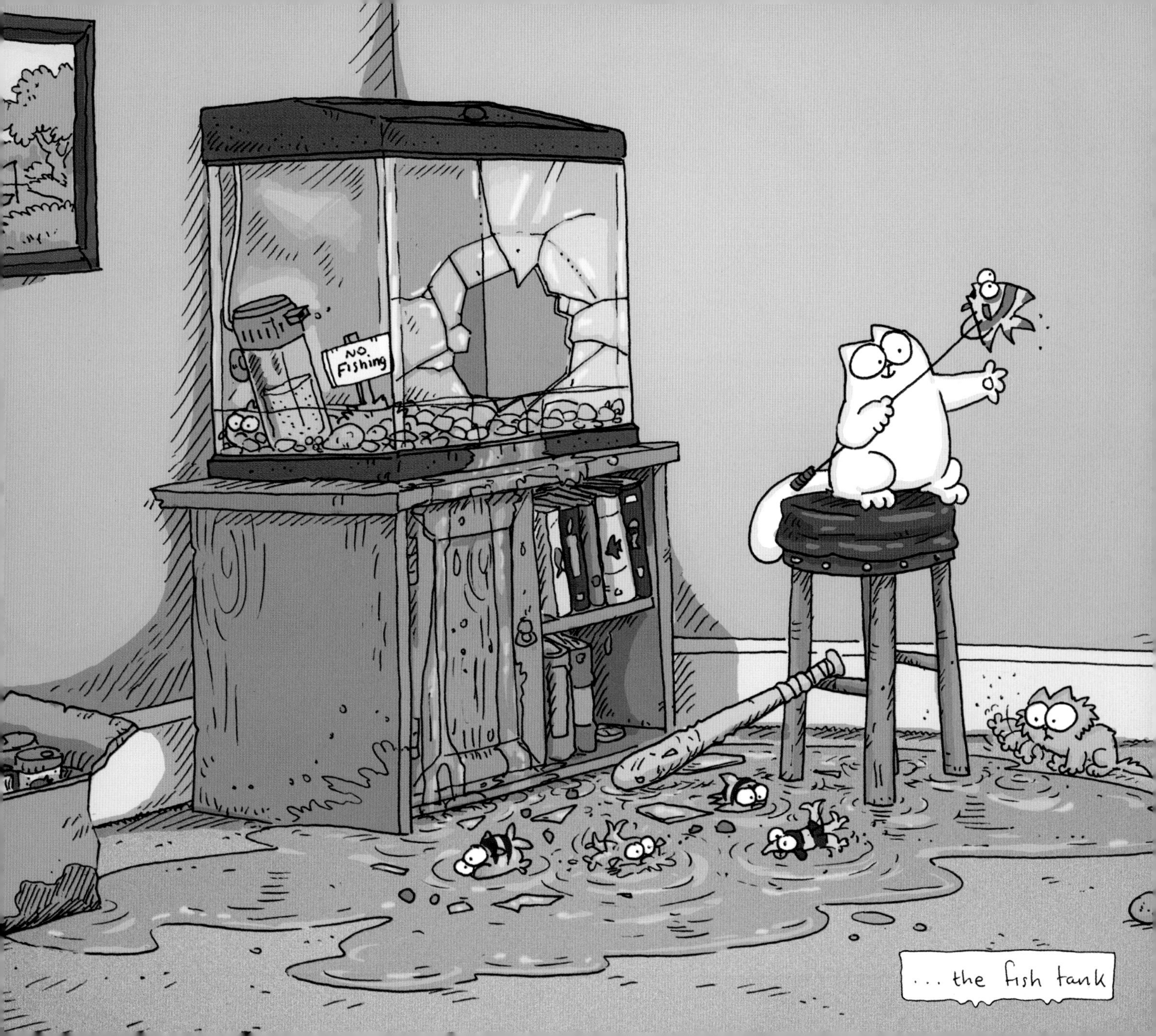
NO Fishing
... the fish tank

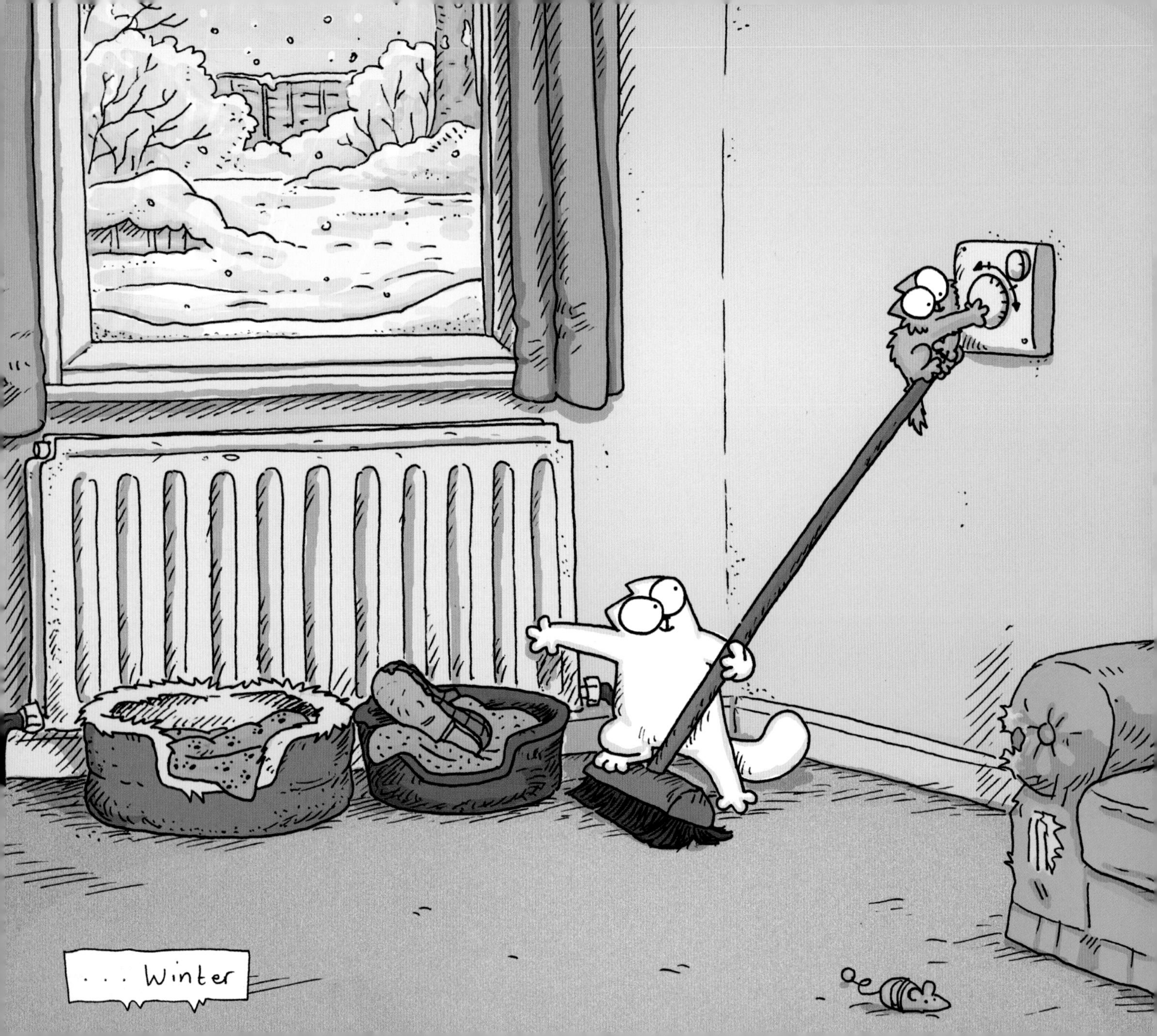
. . . Winter

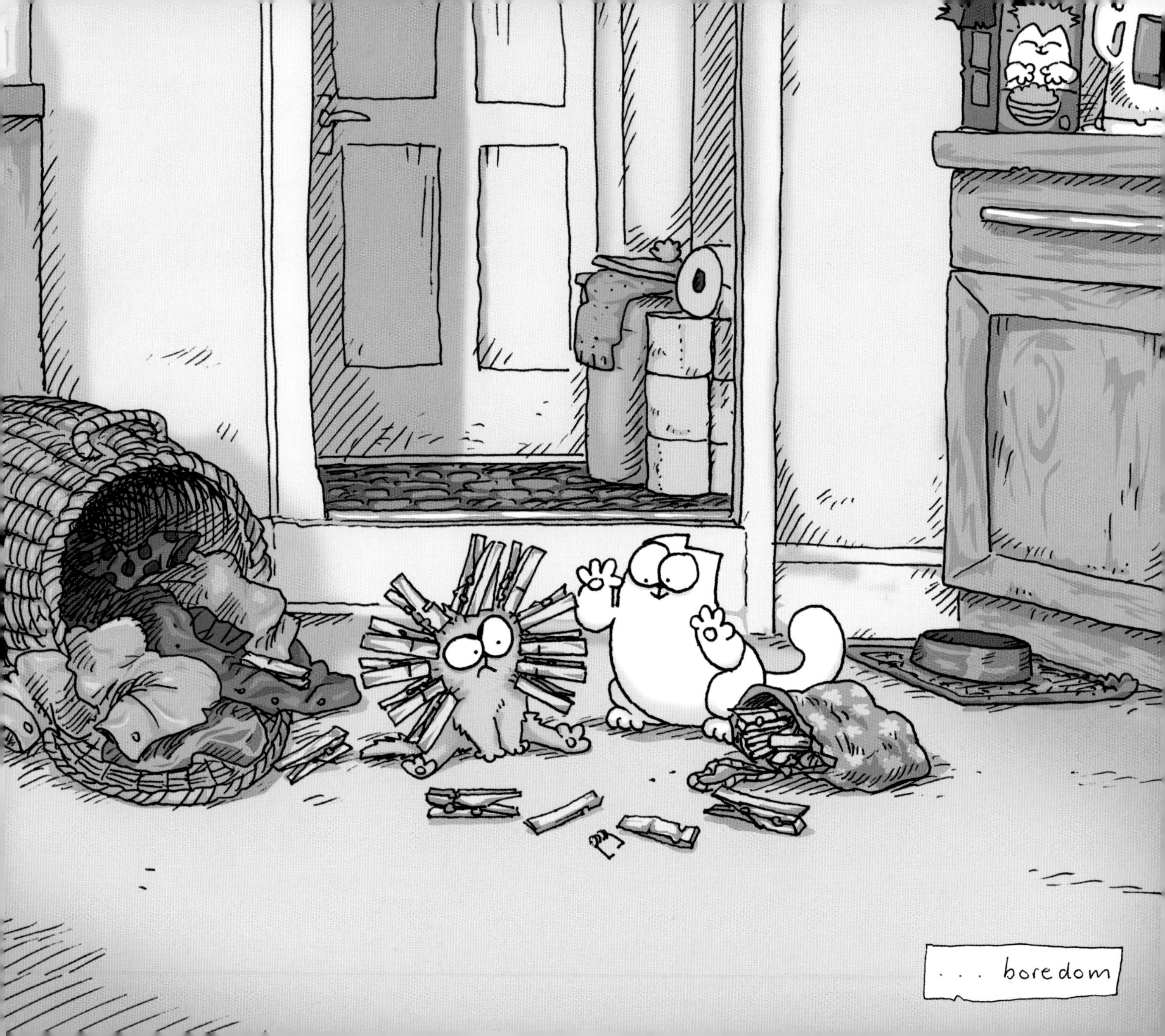
. . . boredom

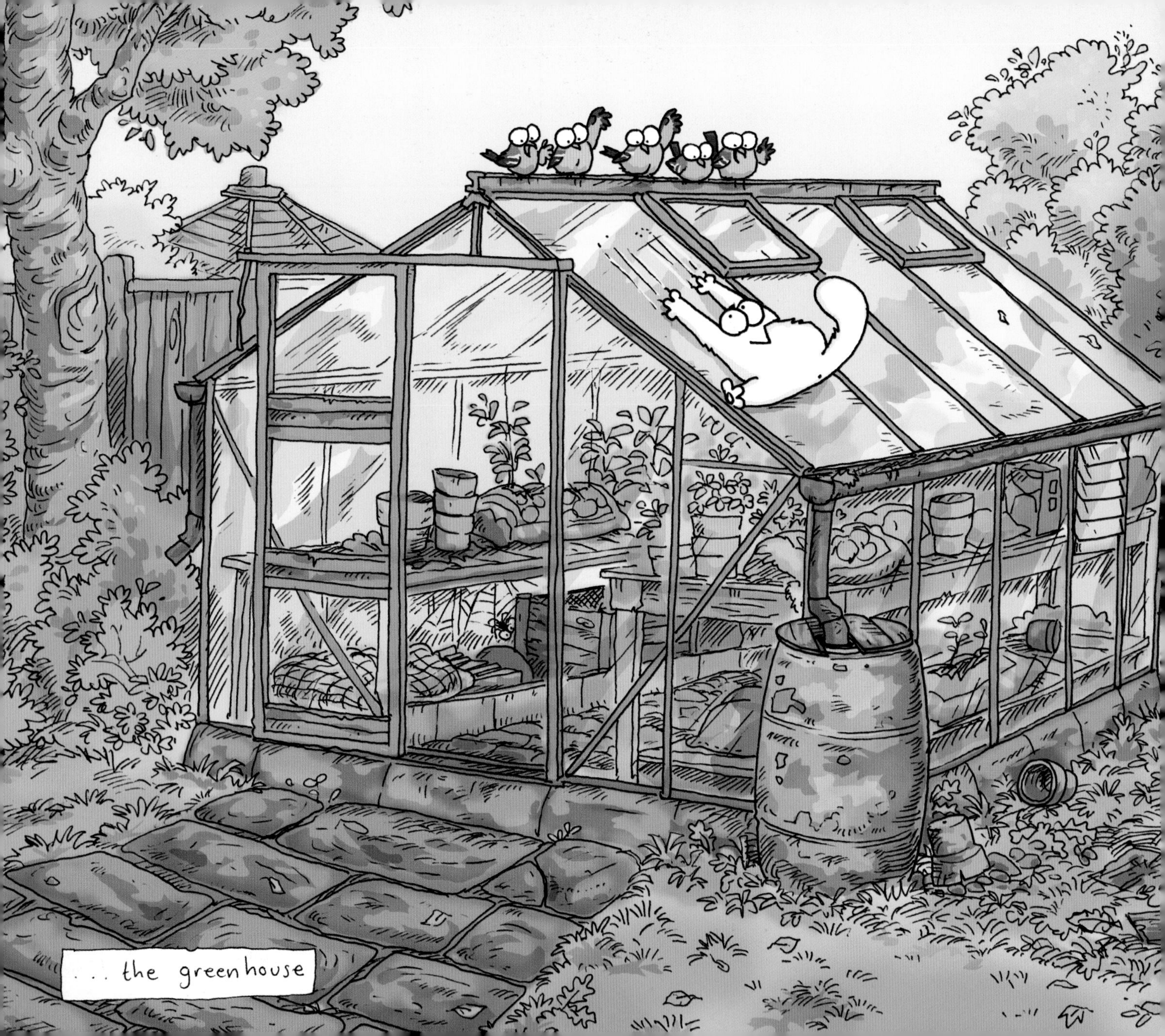

. . . the greenhouse

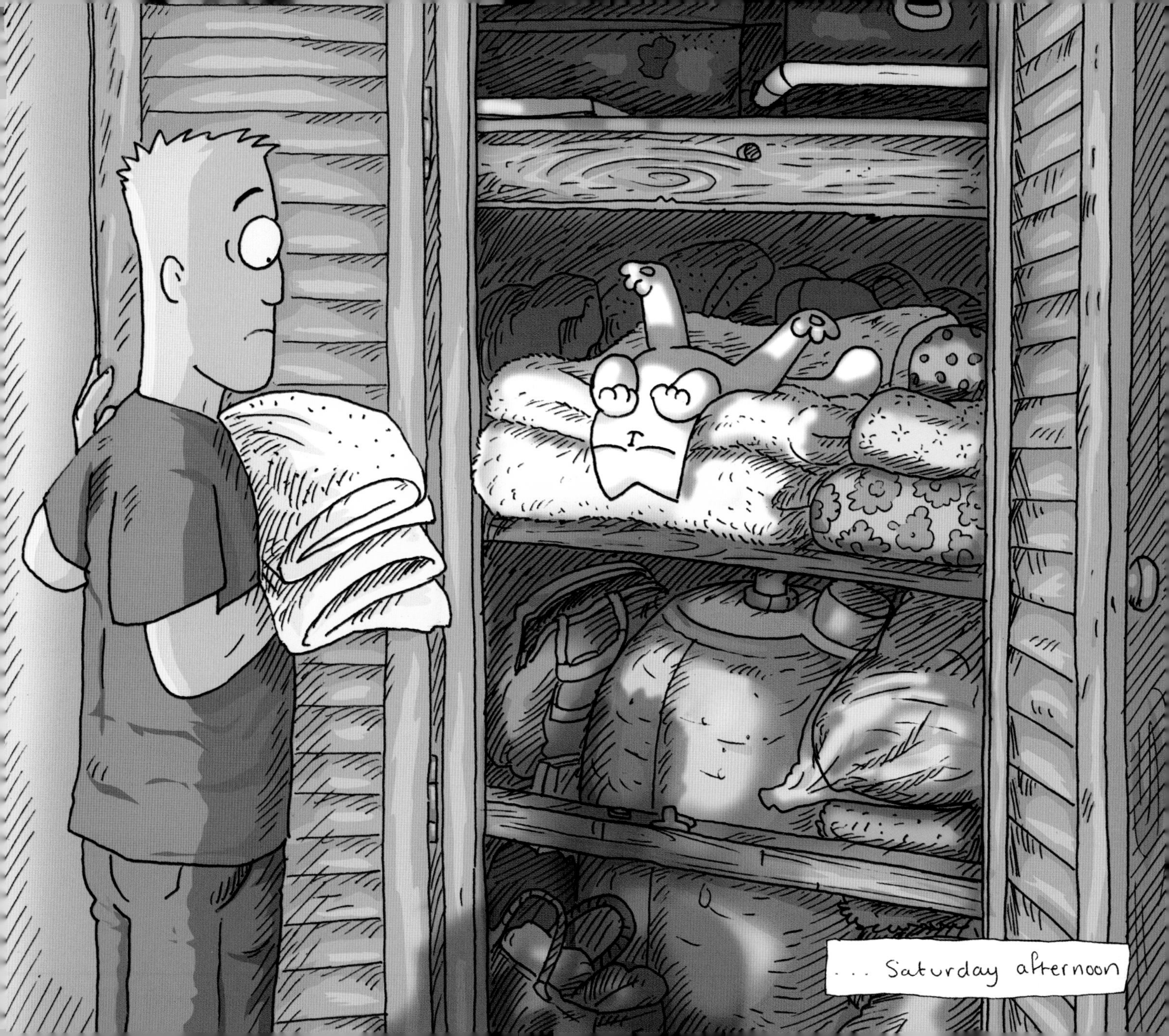
. . . Saturday afternoon

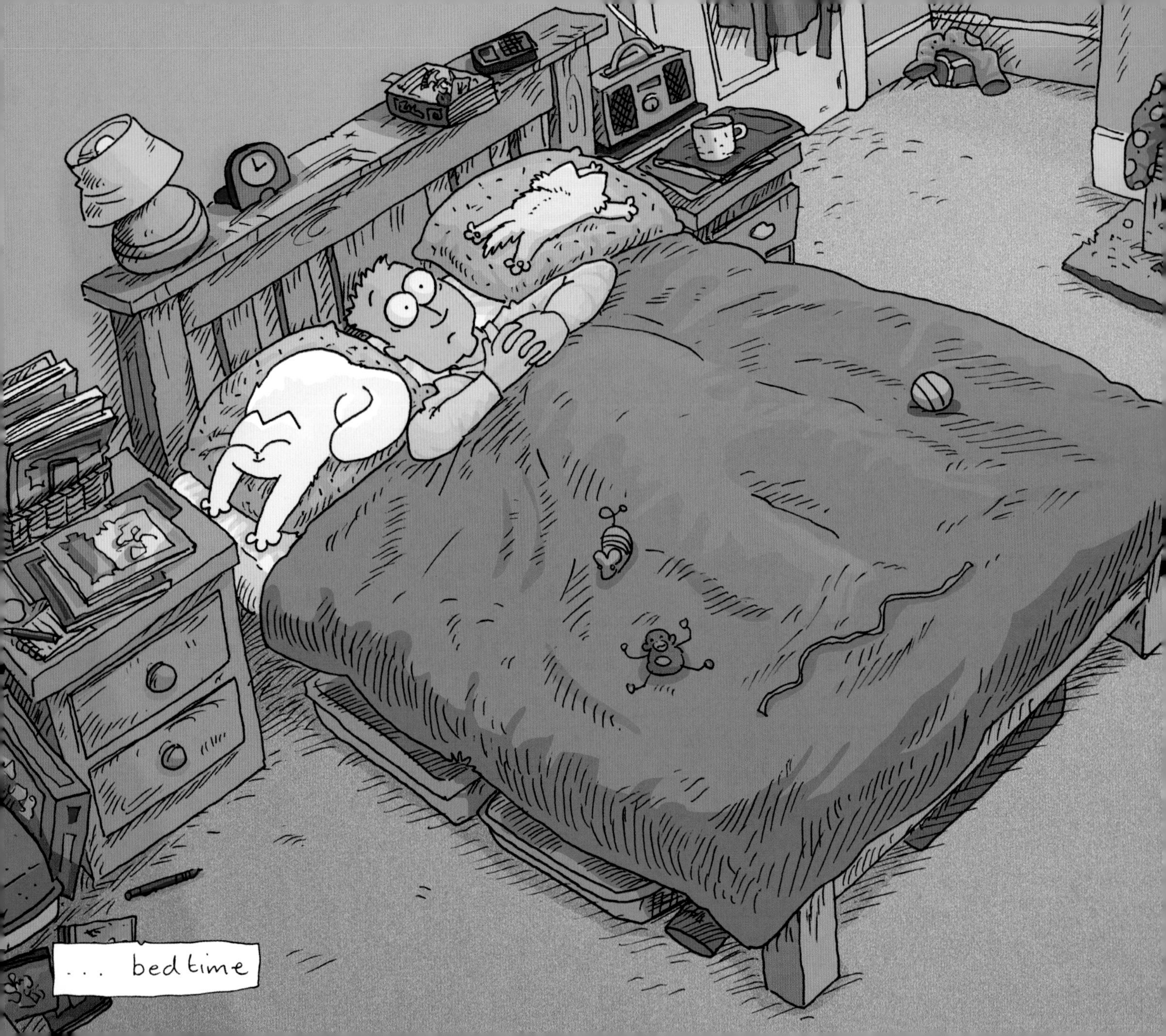
. . . bed time

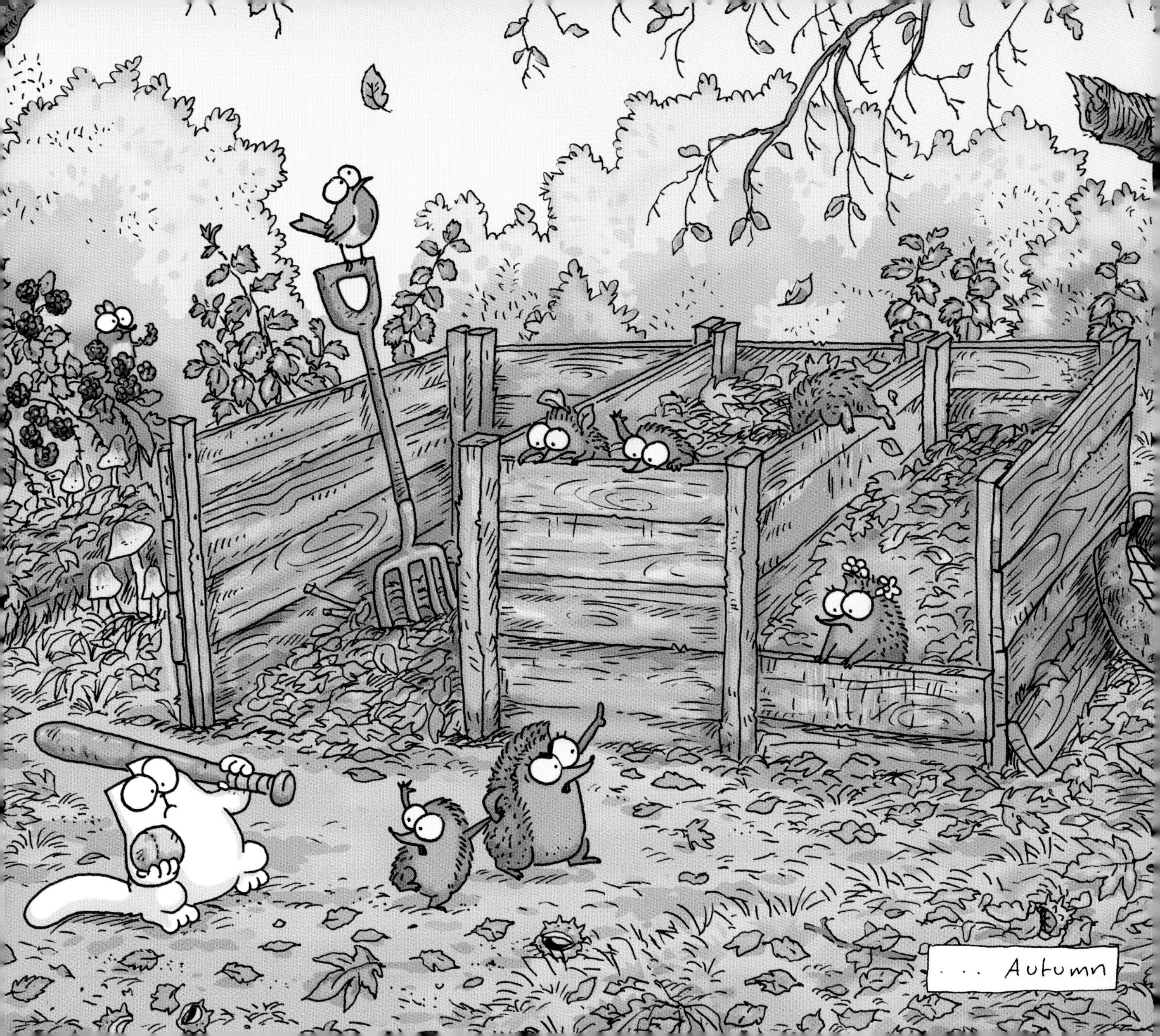
. . . Autumn

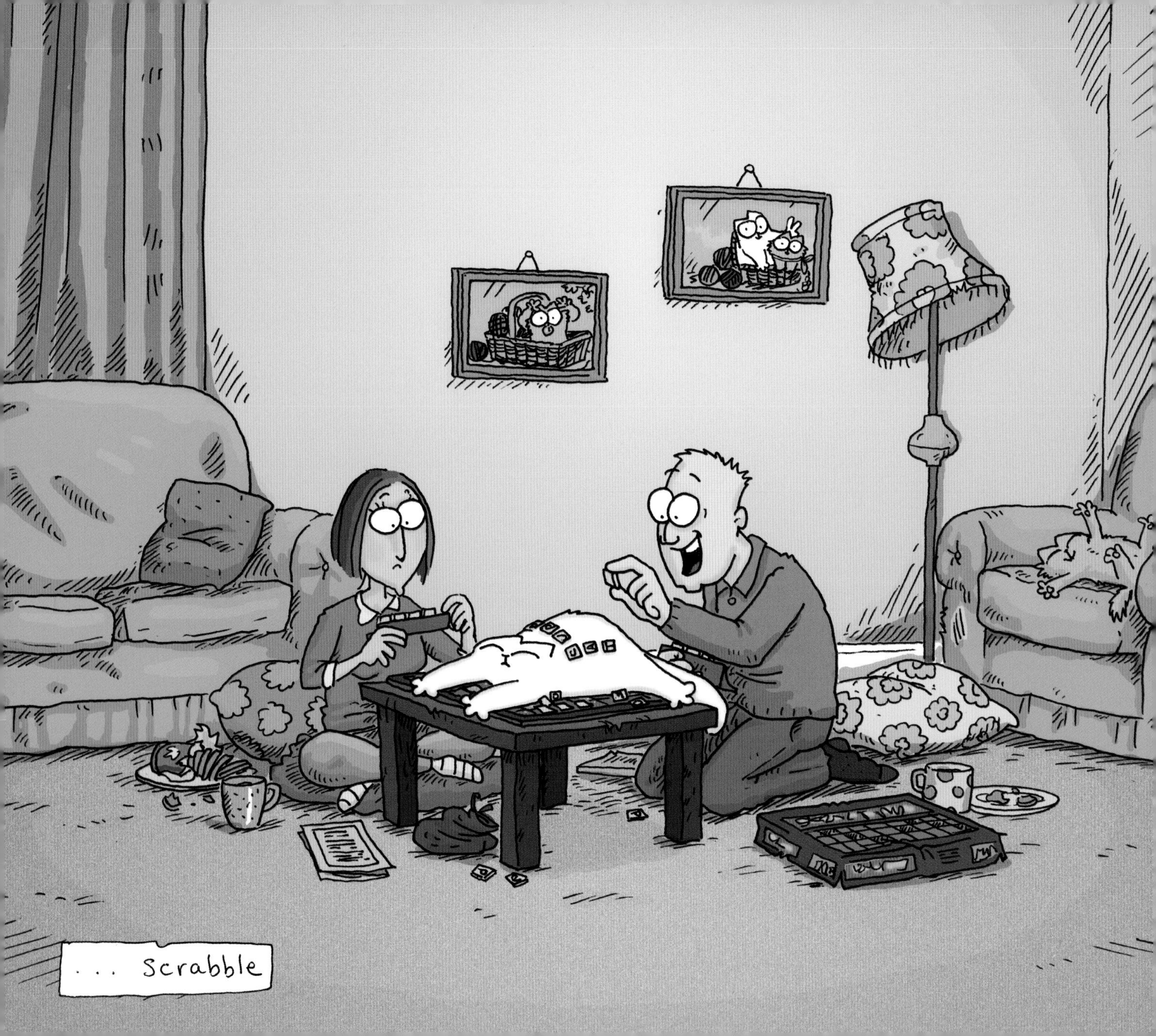

... Scrabble

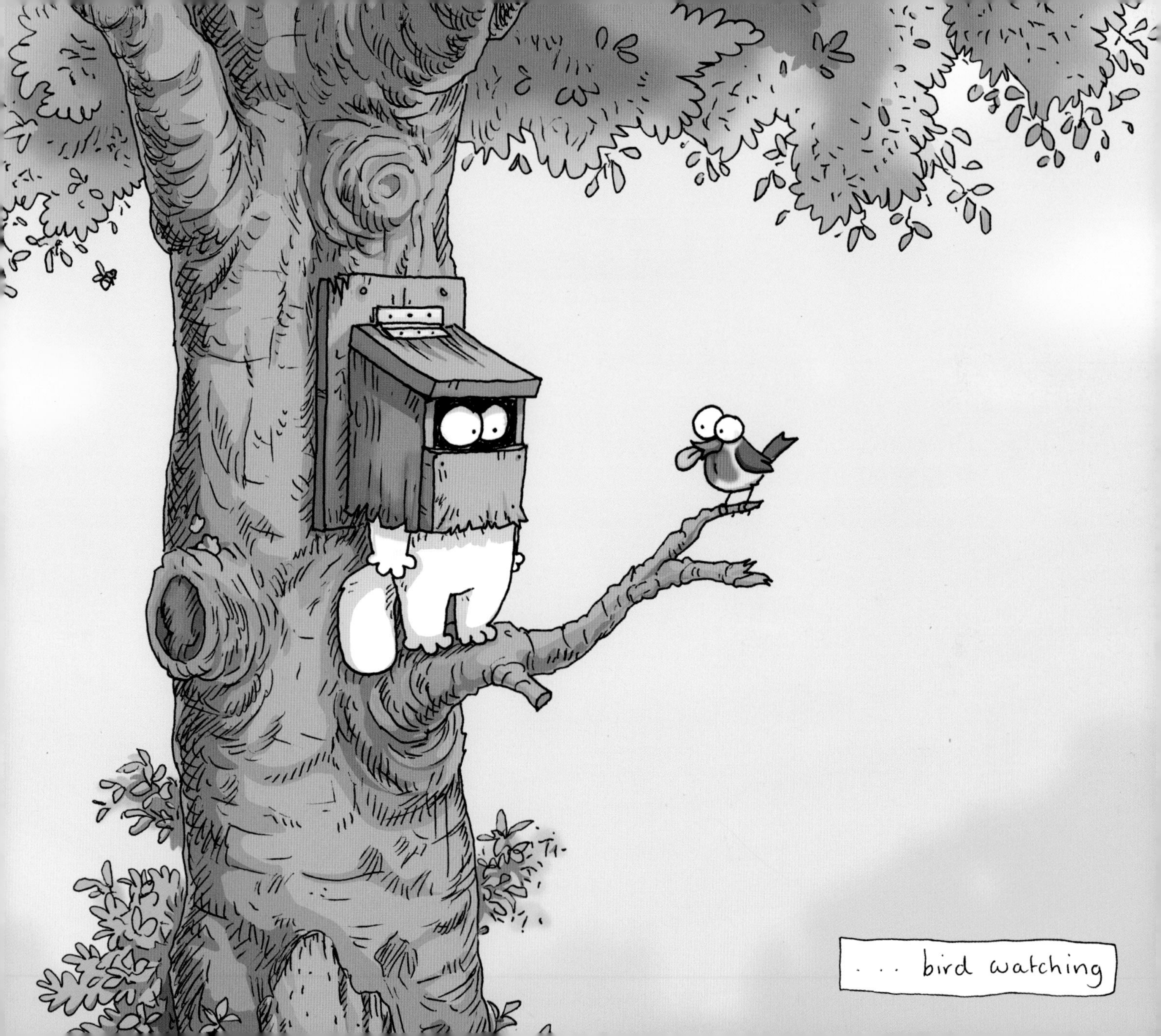

. . . bird watching

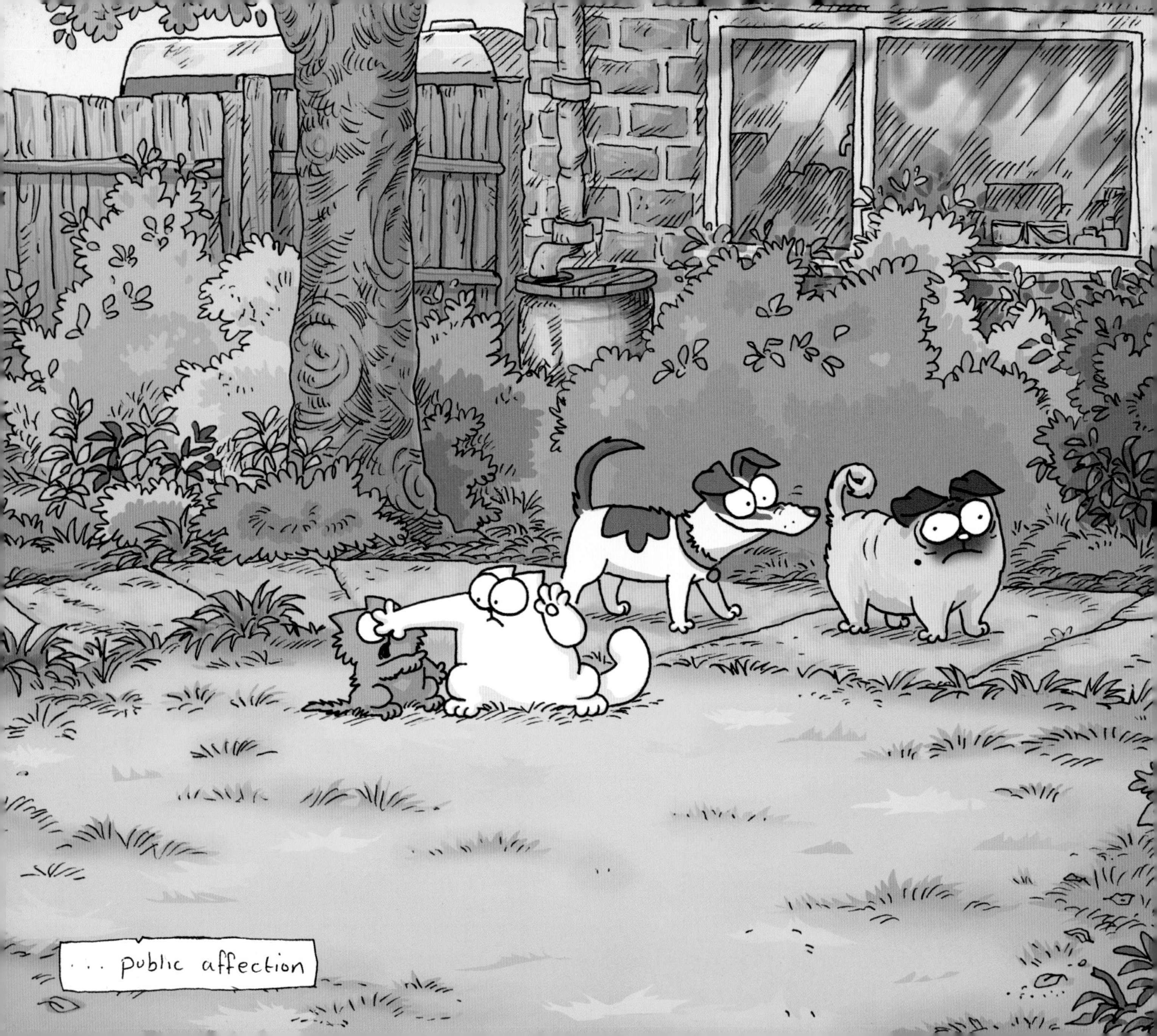
. . . public affection

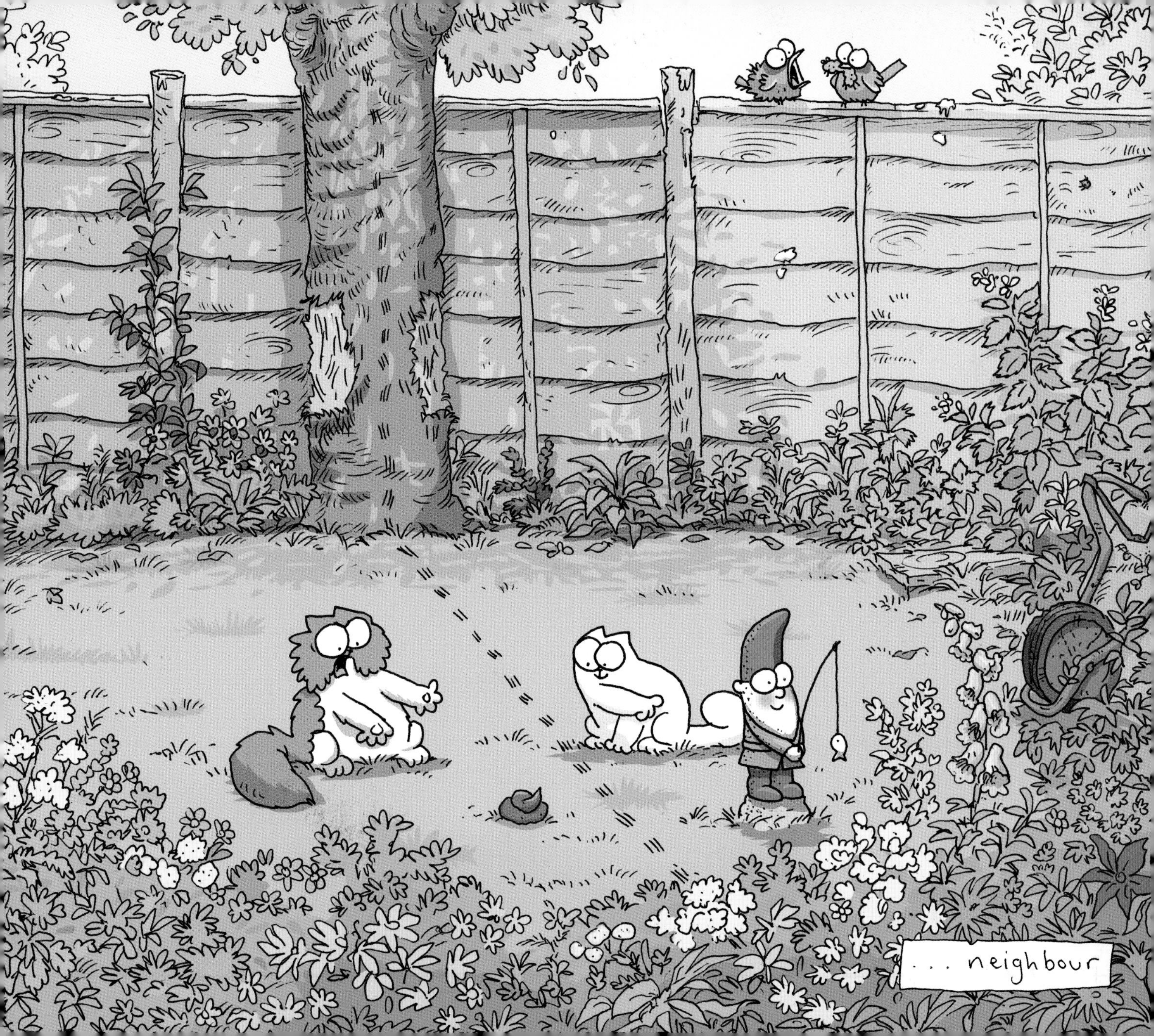
. . . neighbour

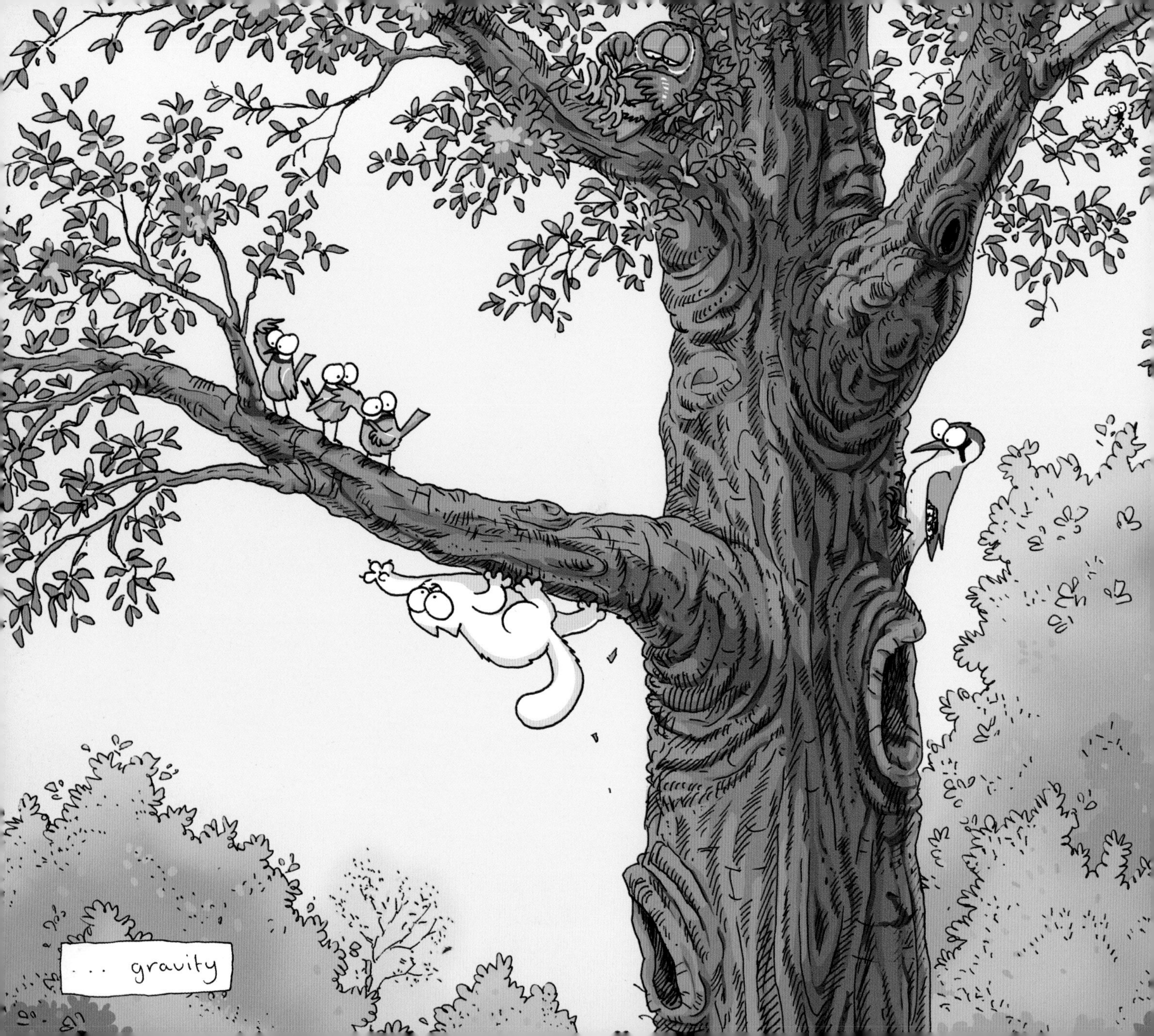
. . . gravity

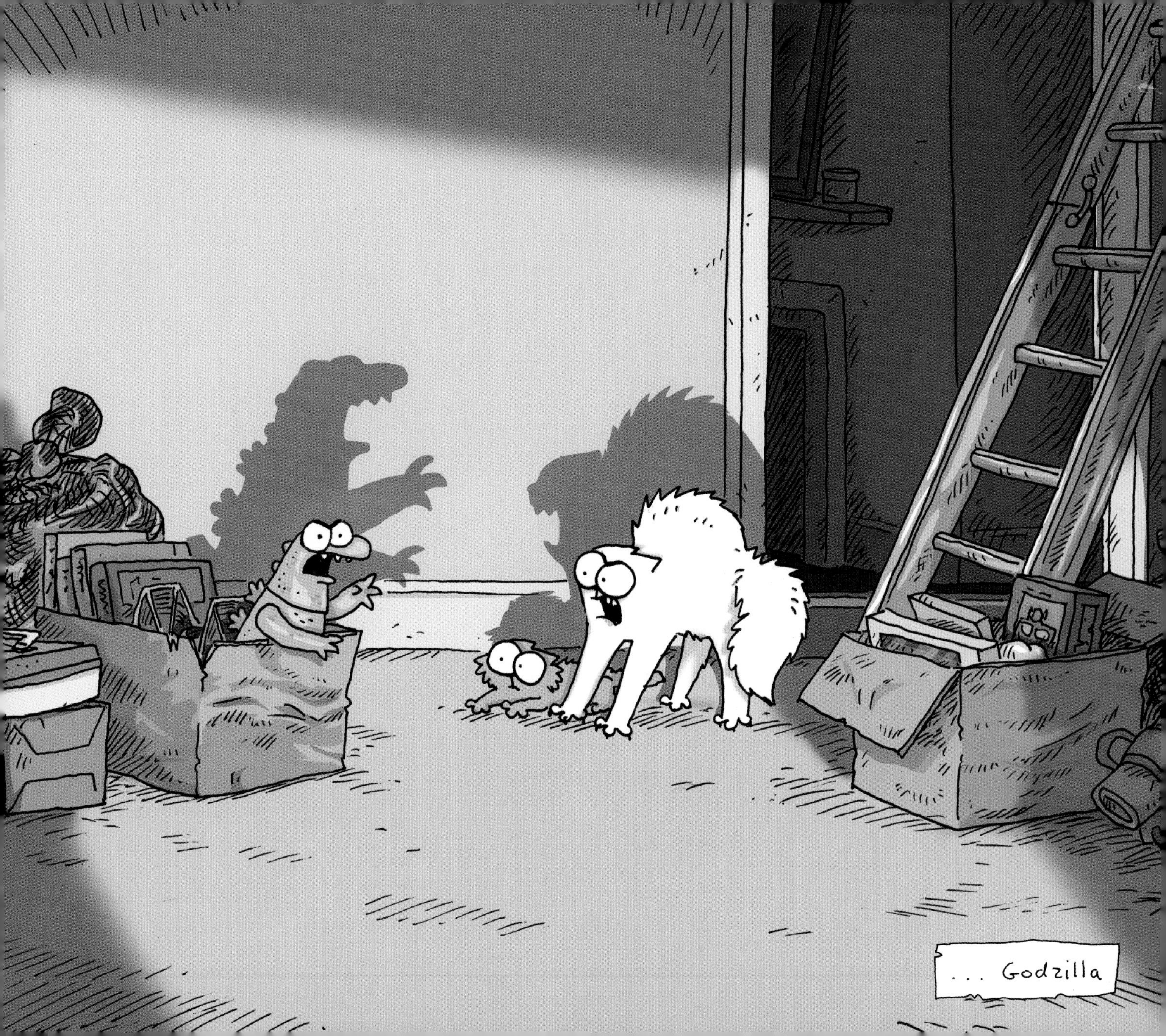
. . . Godzilla

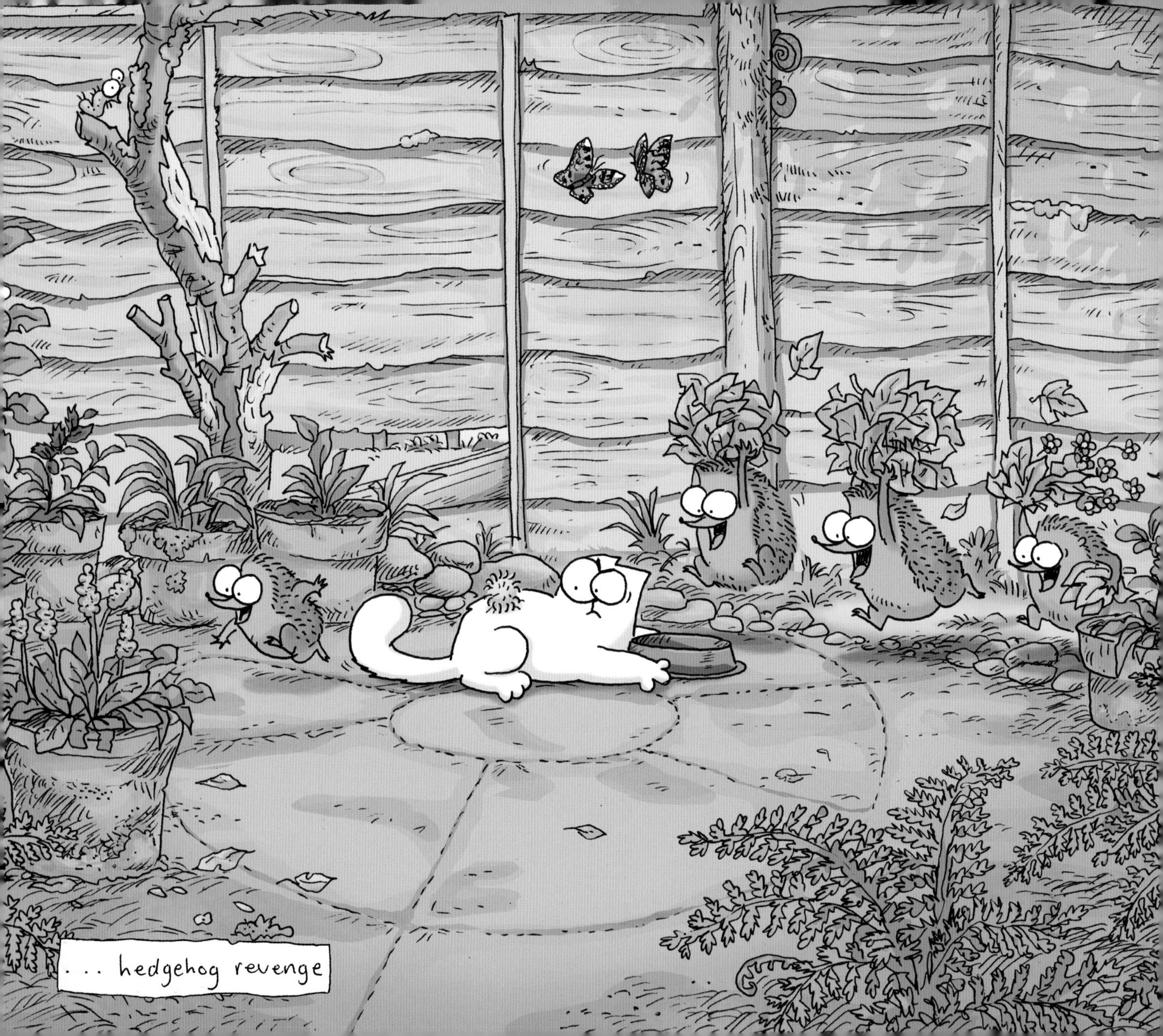
. . . hedgehog revenge

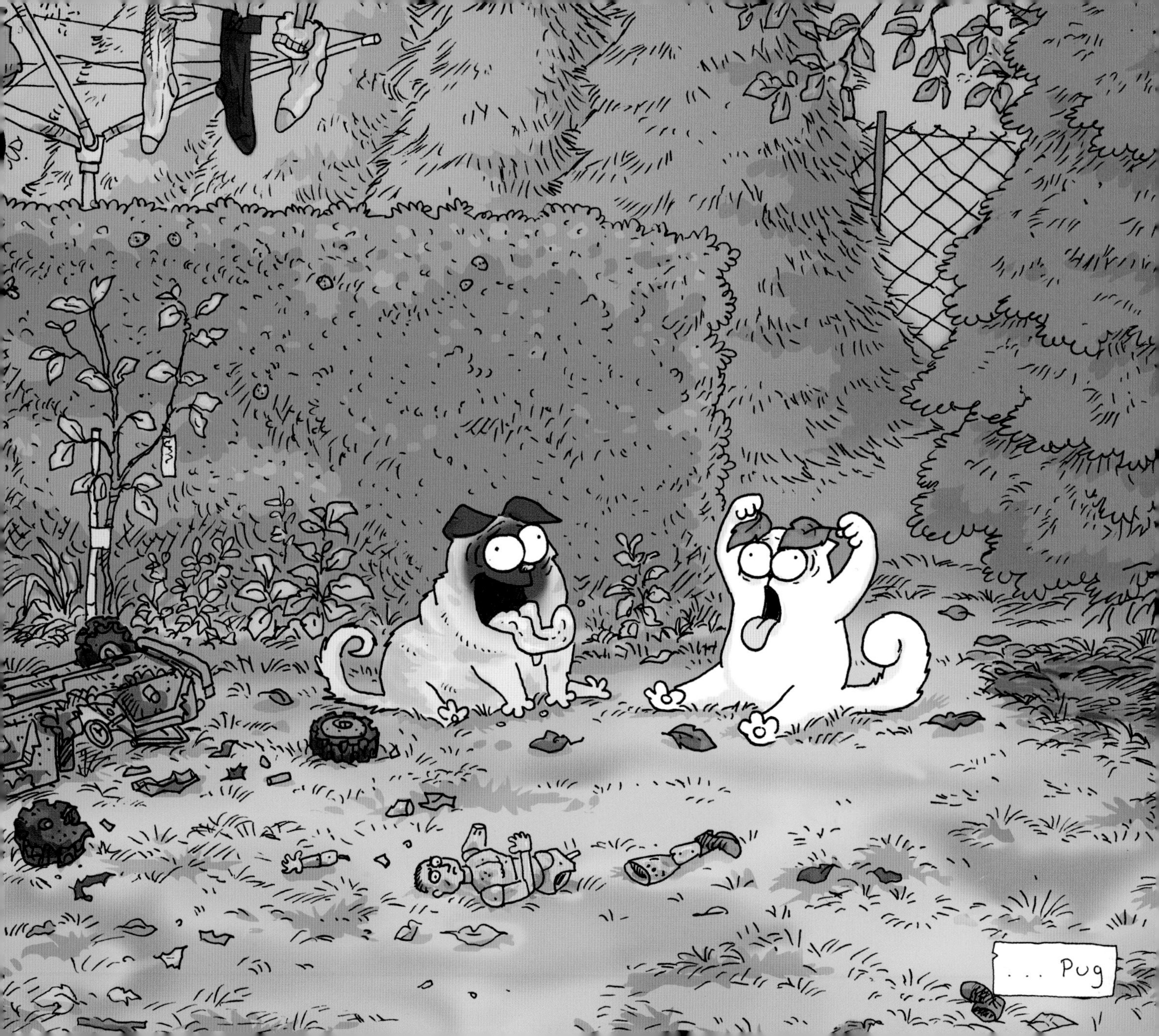
. . . Pug

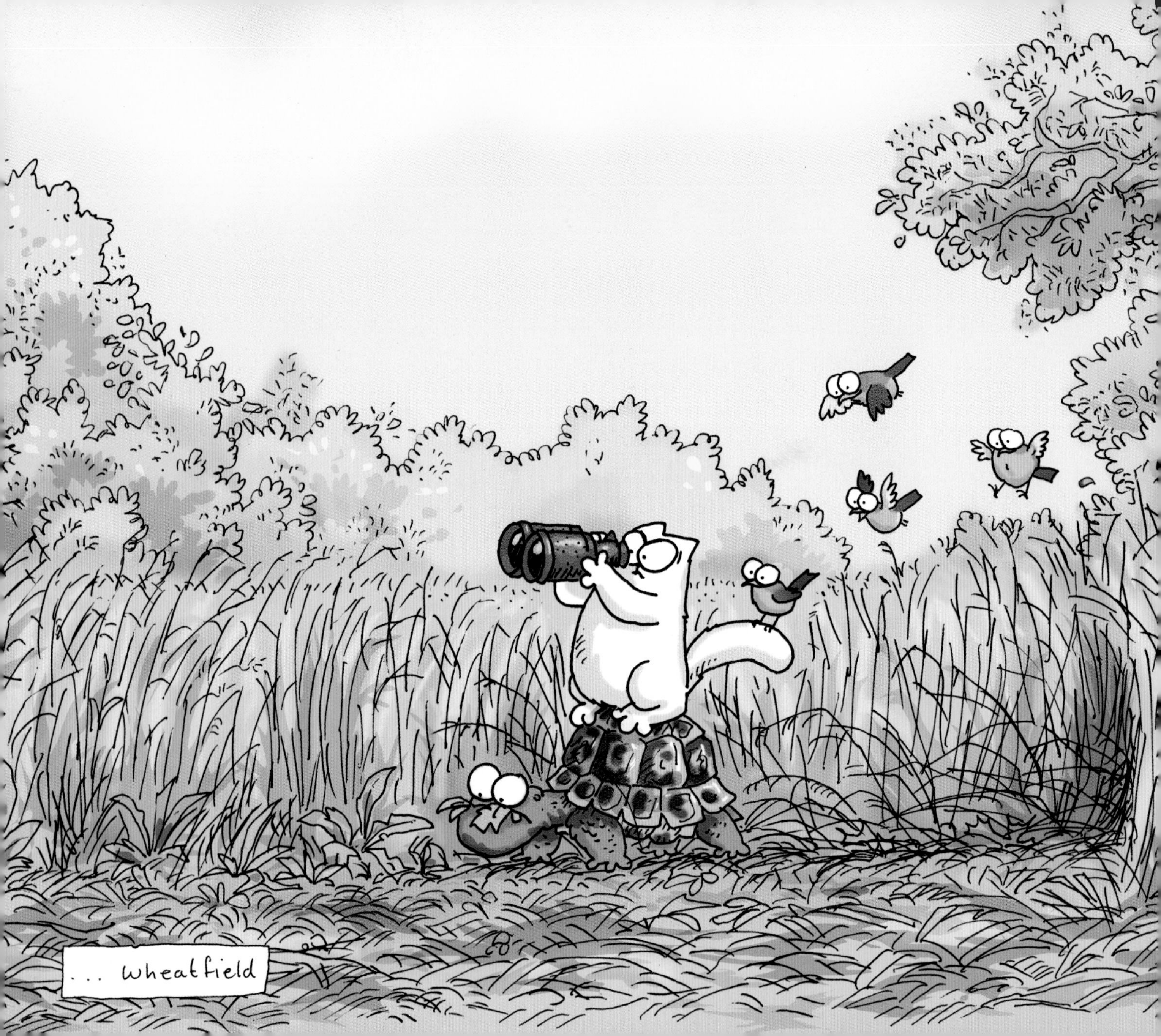
... wheatfield

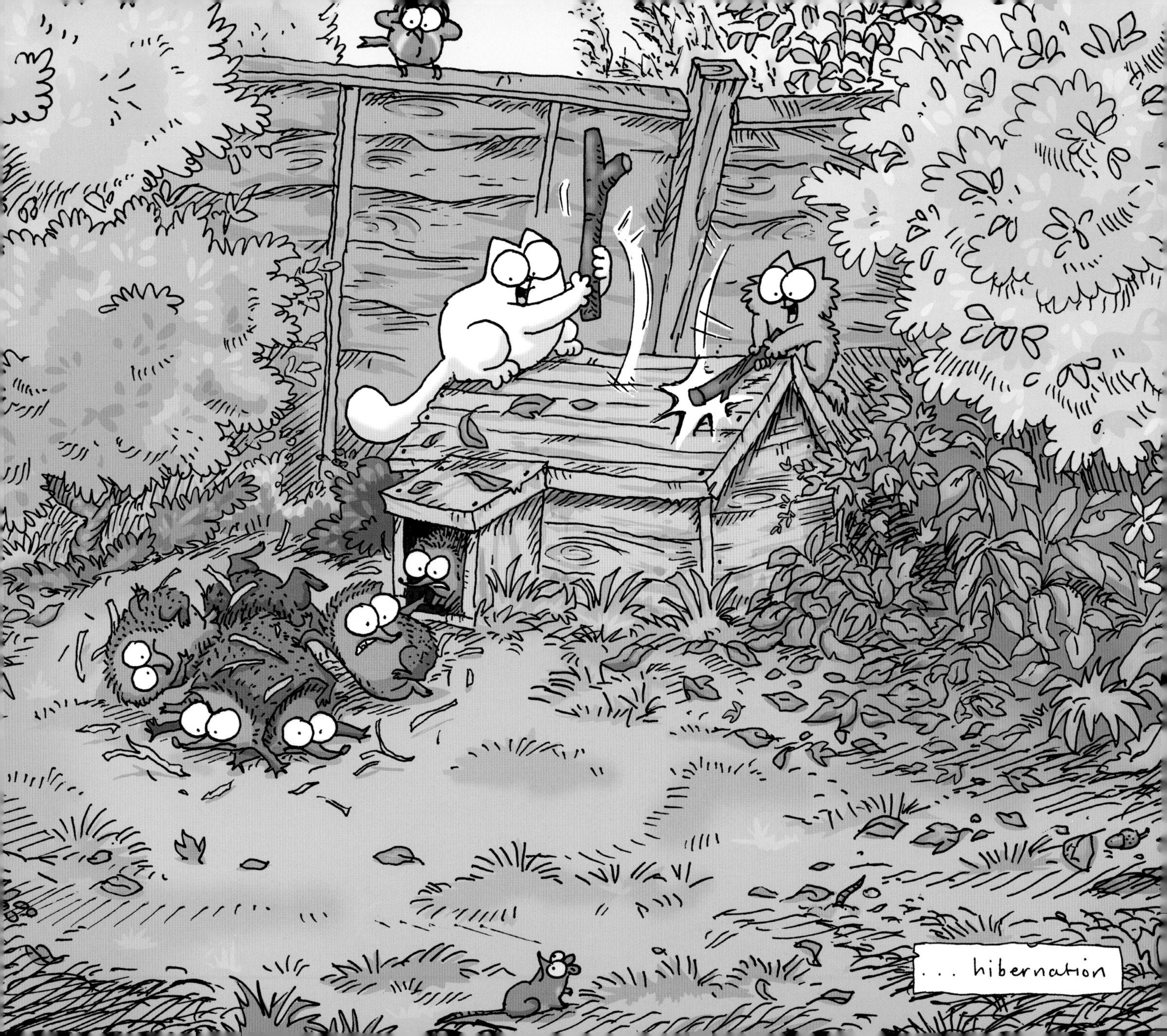
. . . hibernation

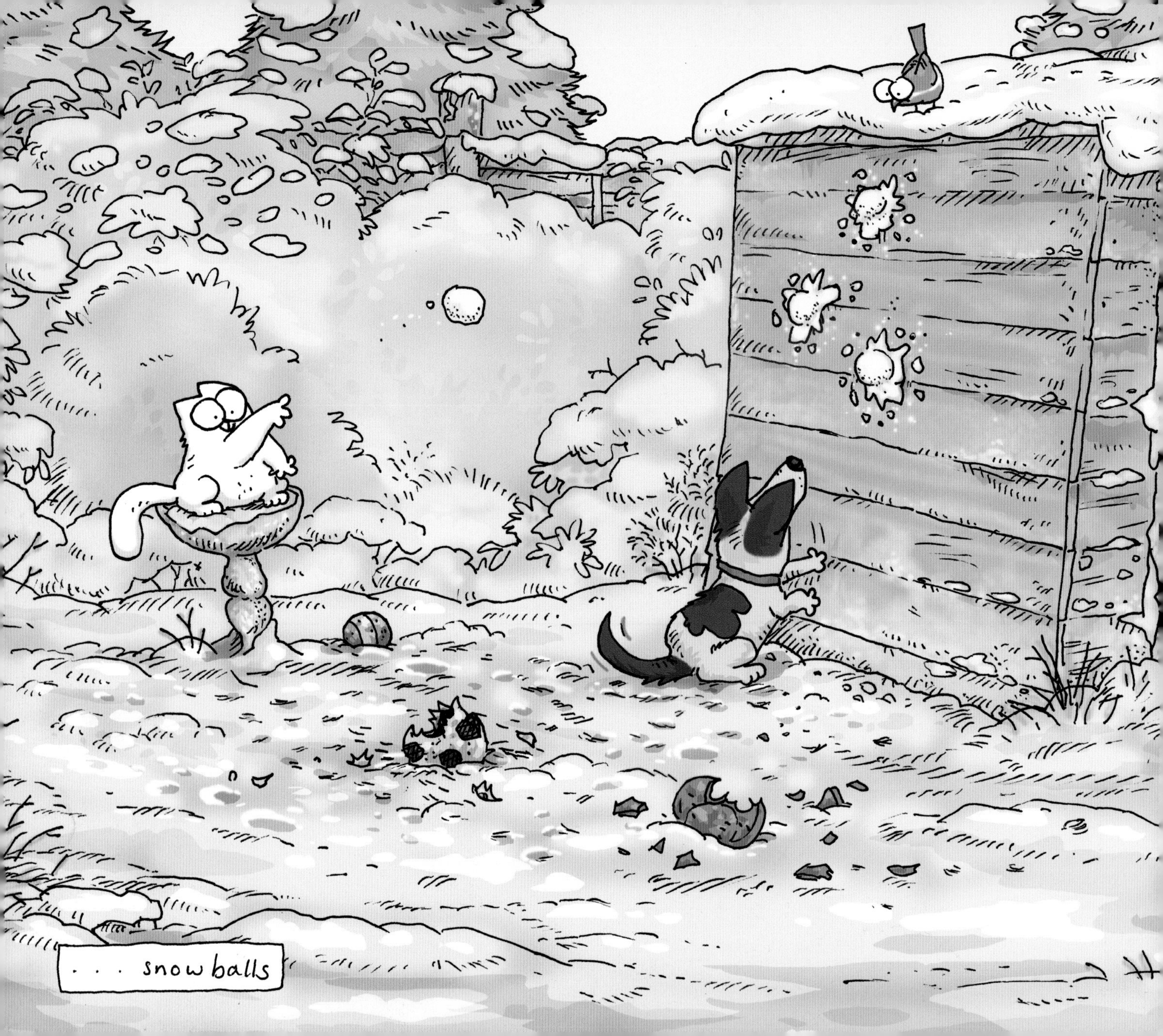
. . . snowballs

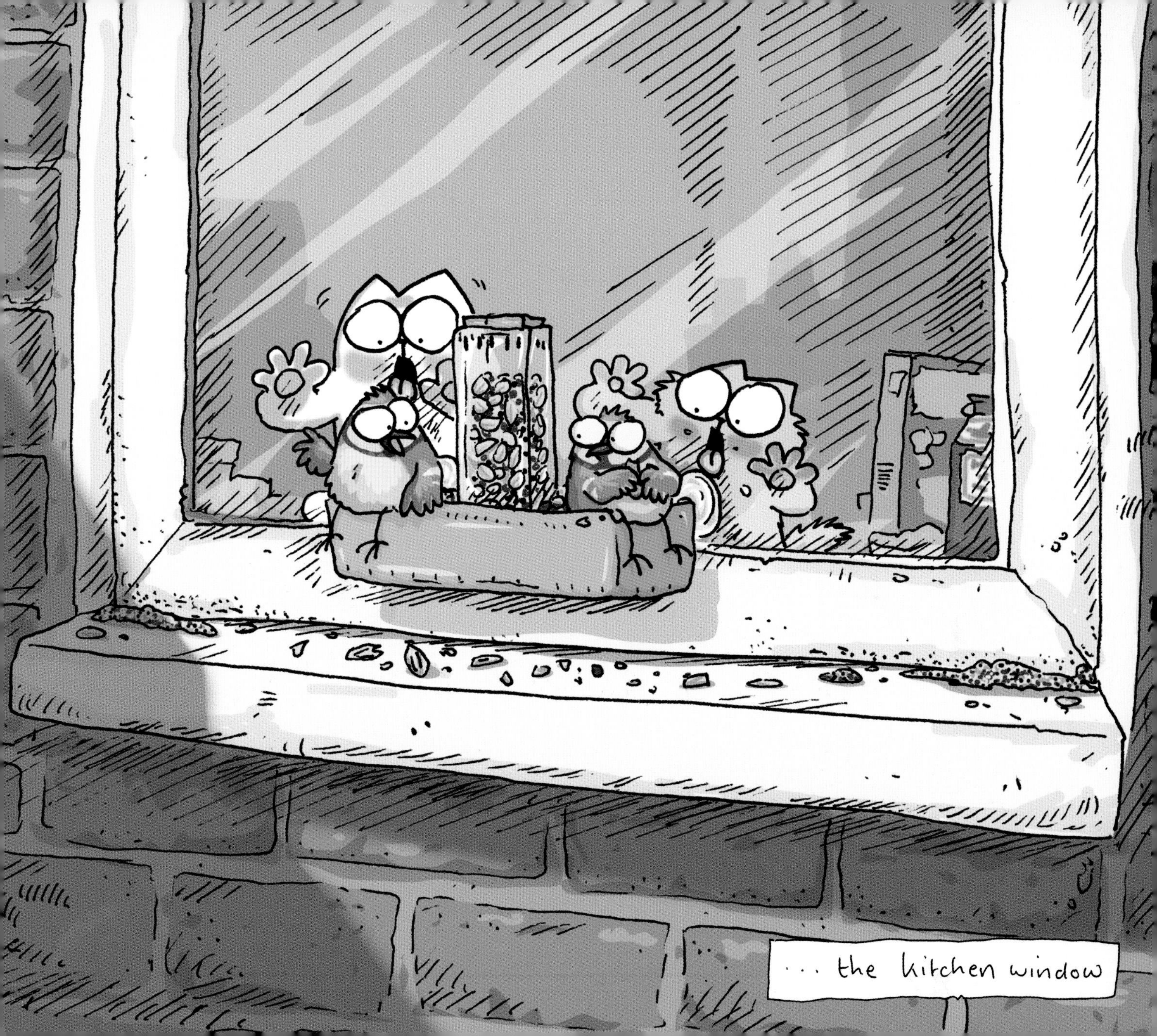
... the kitchen window

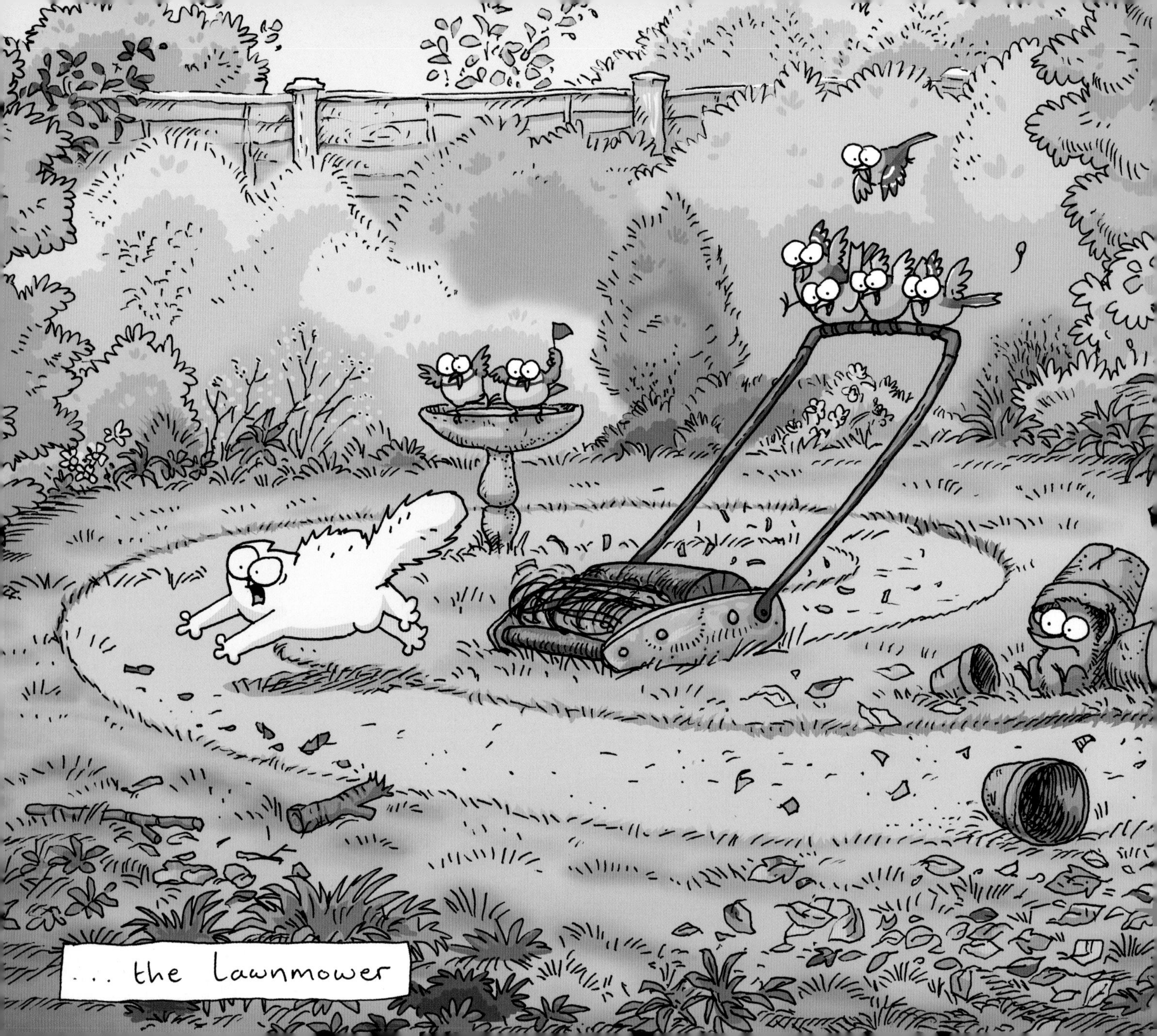
. . . the lawnmower

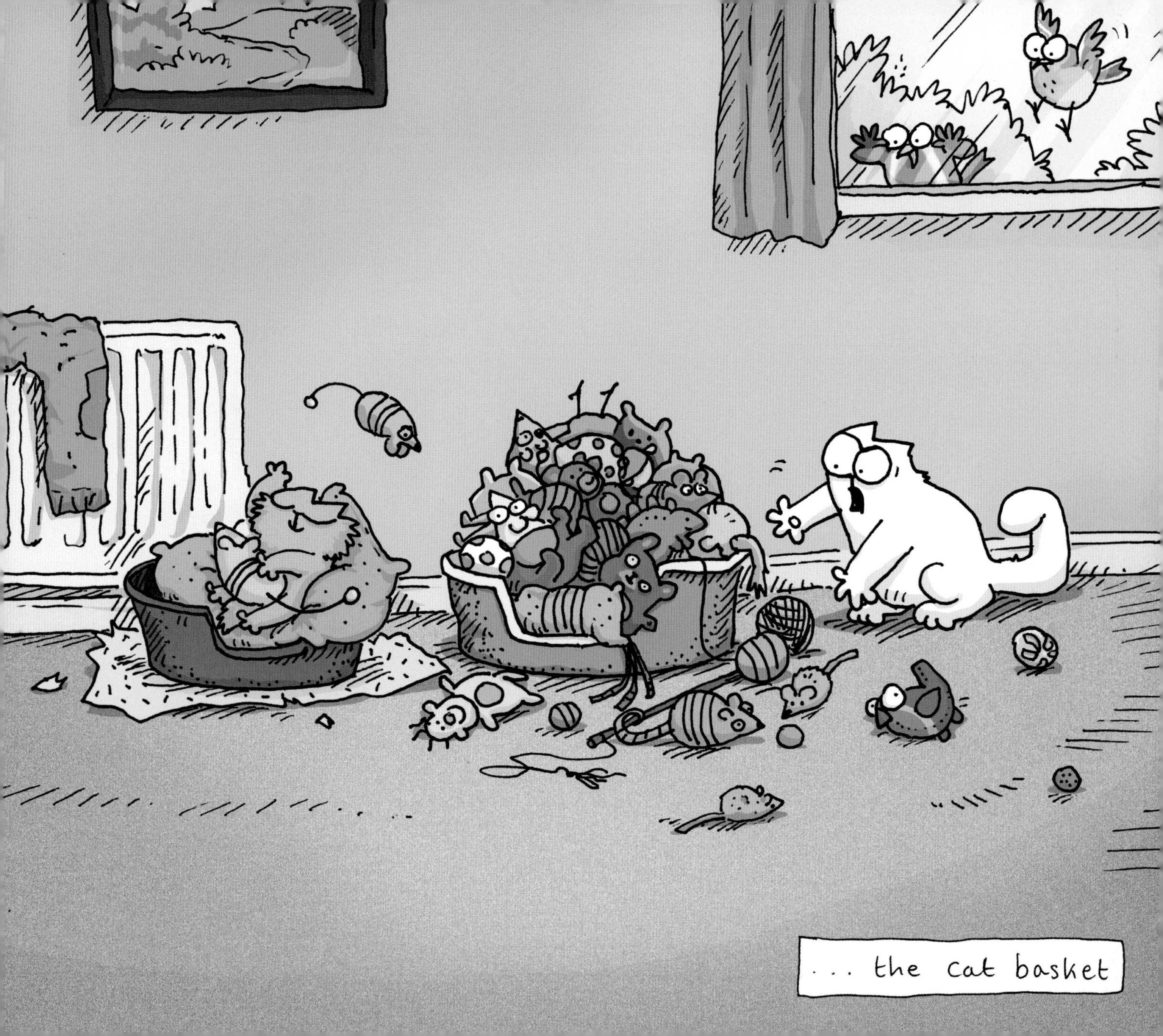

. . . the cat basket

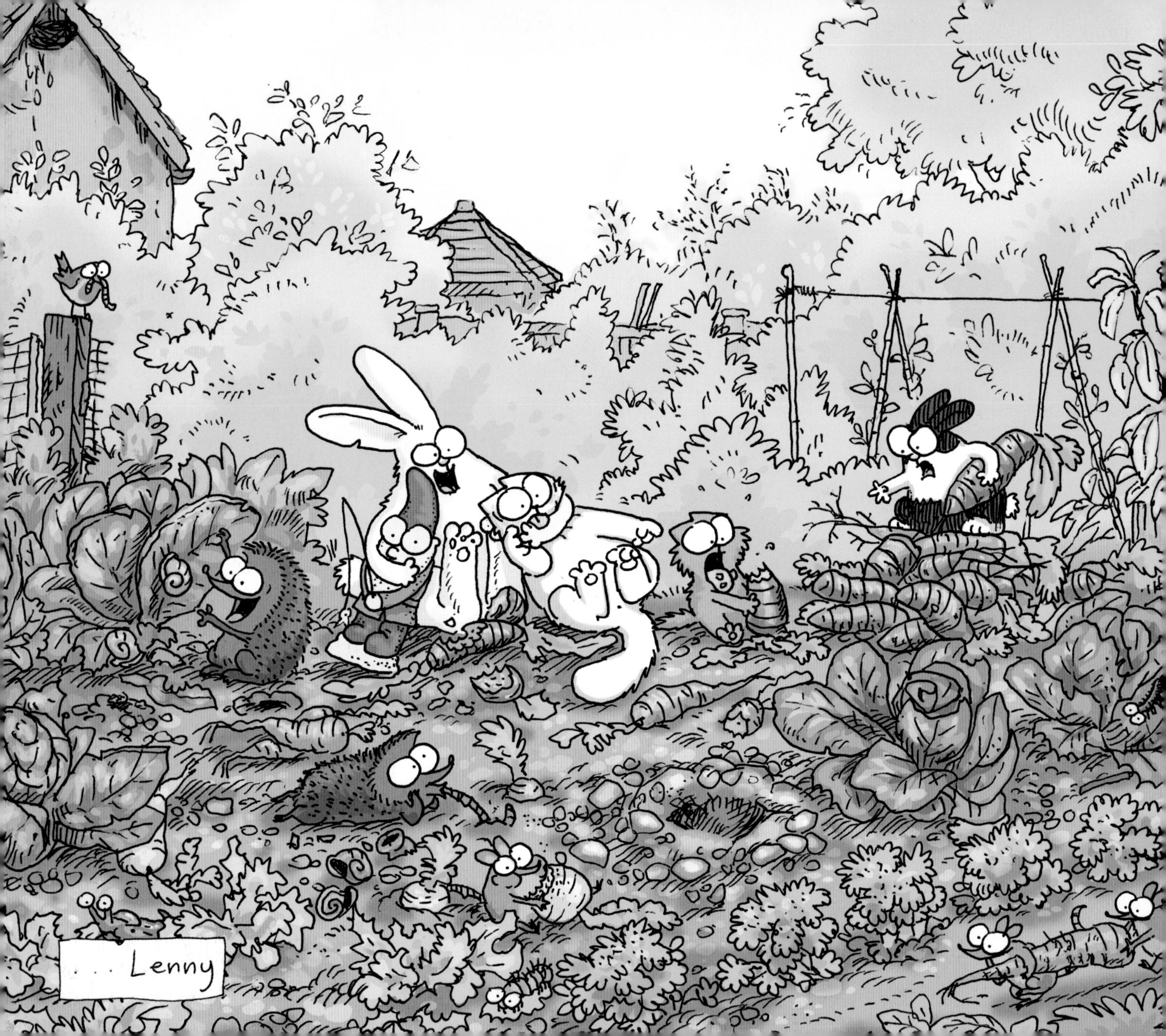
. . . Lenny

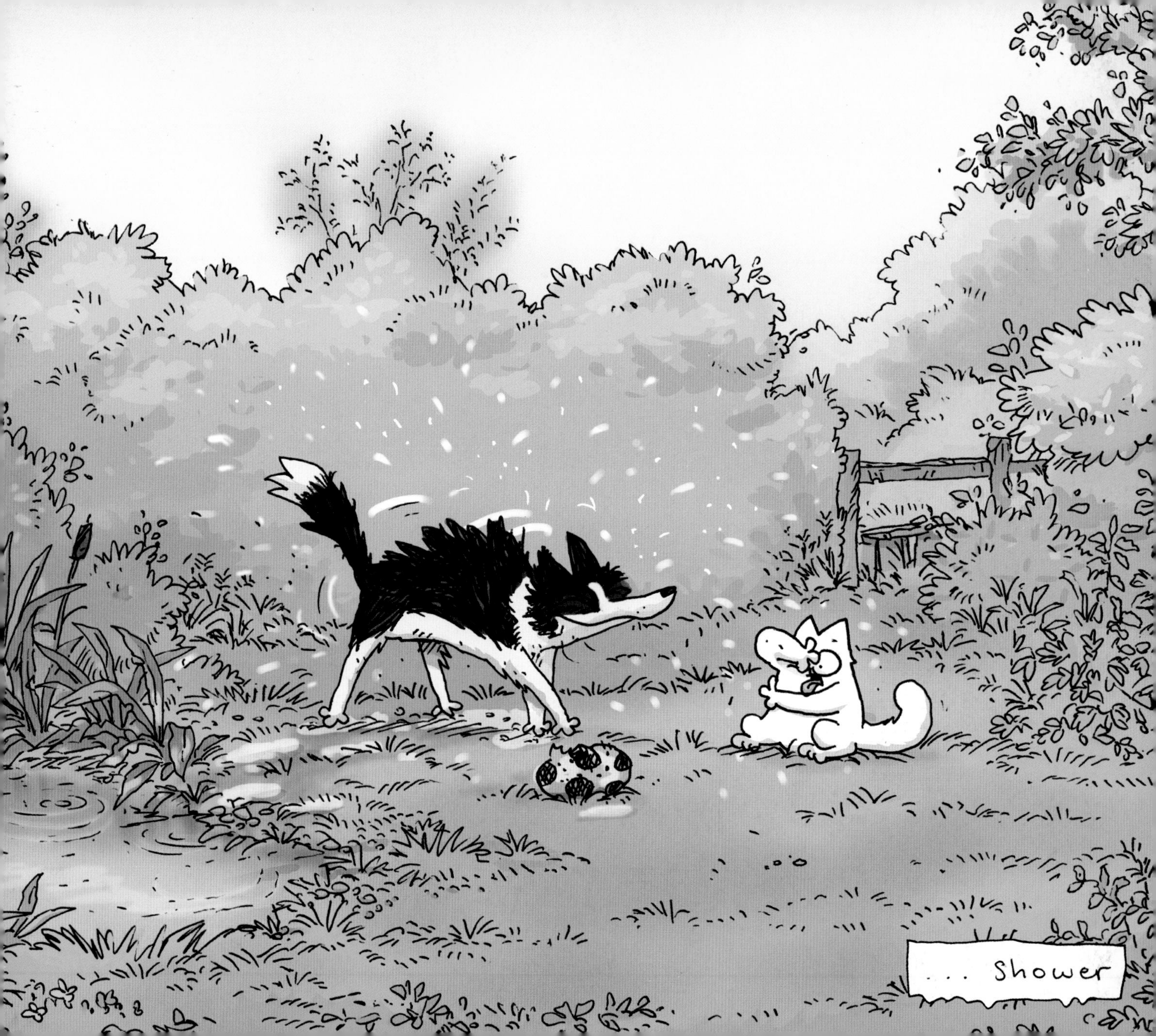
. . . Shower

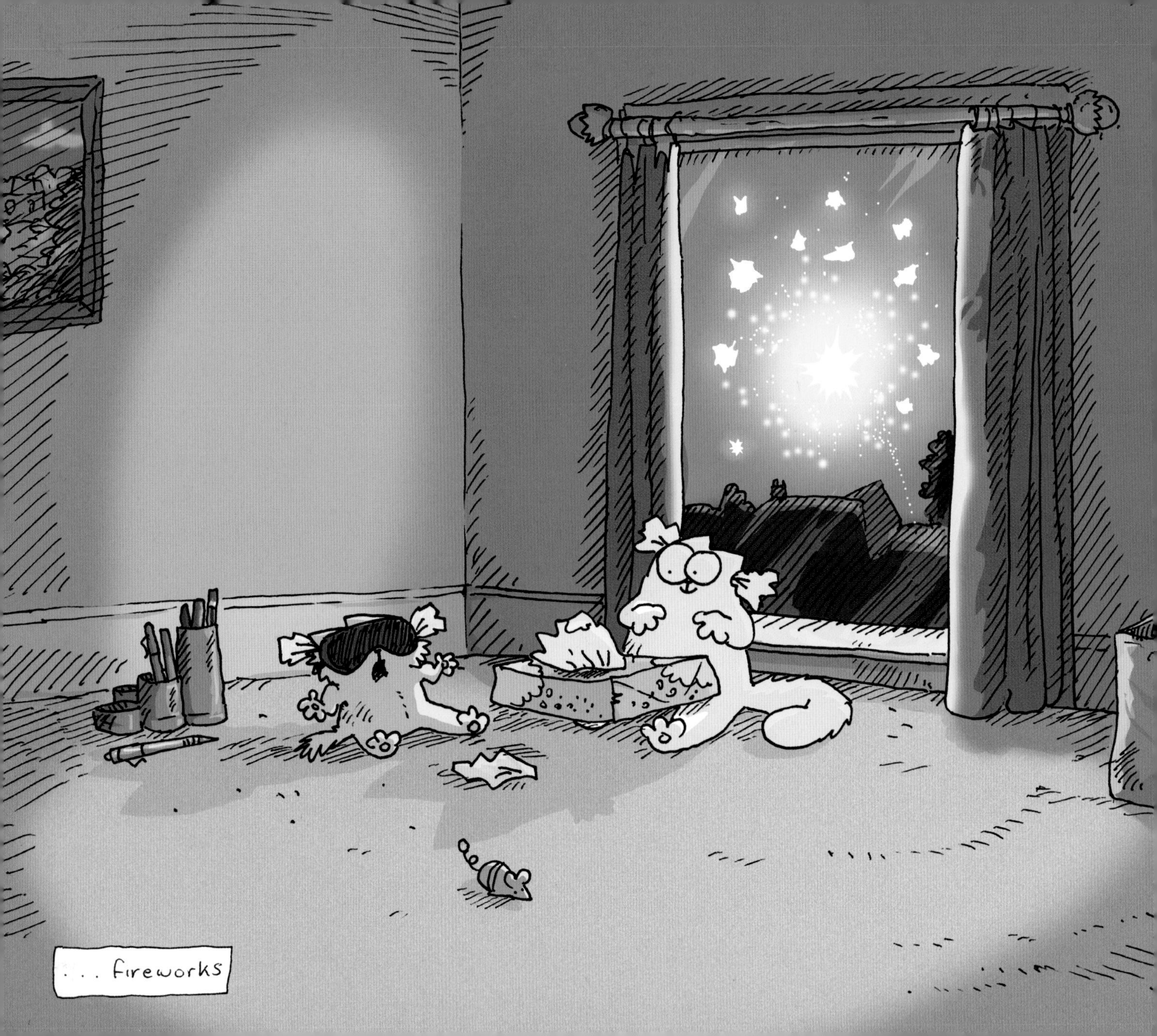
. . . fireworks

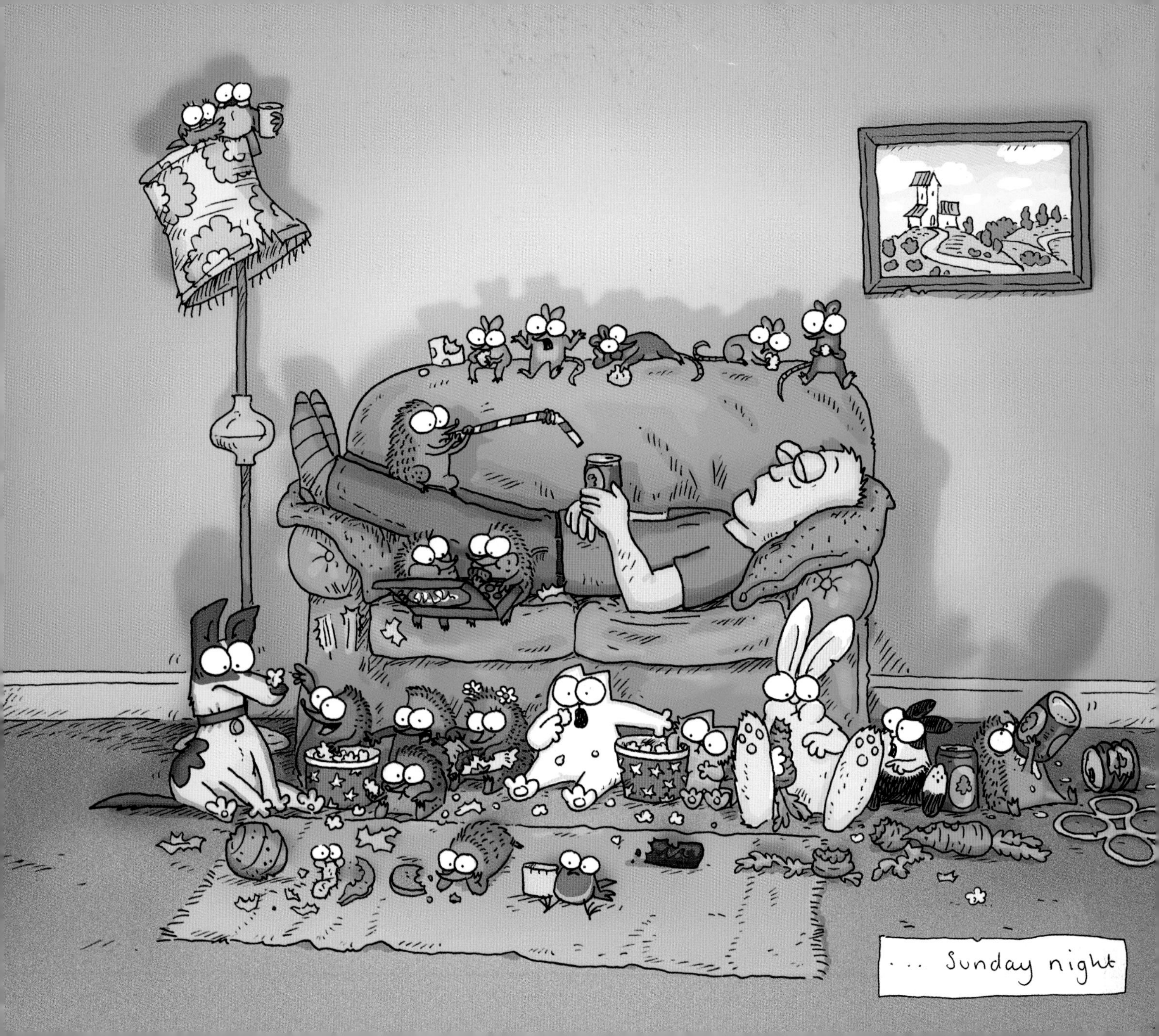
. . . Sunday night

Simon Draws : A Siamese Cat

1:

Let's start with two big almond-shaped eyes,.

2:

There are big M-shaped ears and a little nose.

3:

Siamese cats have very elegant long necks so I taper the neck in.

4:

Then I draw tiny little paws on long legs.

5:

I continue the back to make a little bottle-shaped body and a tiny rear foot.

6:

Instead of a fat Simon's Cat tail there is a long thin tail.

7:

Siamese cats have very dark faces. But I'm only going to shade in the ears so you can still see the face.

8:

The tail is also very dark on Siamese cats. So I've shaded that in too.

Simon Draws : A Persian Cat

1:

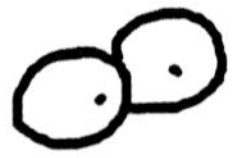

With the Persian cat we start with two big round eyes.

2:

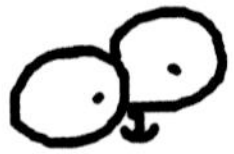

Next I draw a little nose and mouth.

3:

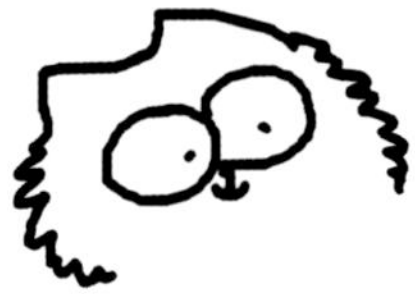

Persian cats tend to have little tiny ears, and a big fluffy pair of cheeks.

4:

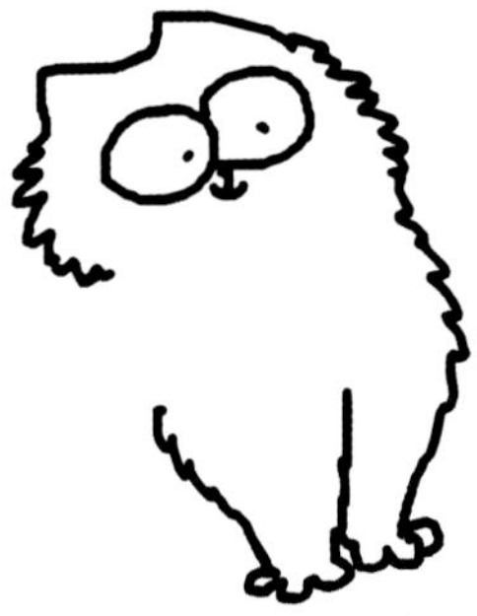

The legs taper down into the feet.

5:

I give him a little bit of a chest and a great big fluffy back.

6:

There's his little rear paw.

7:

Persians are known for their huge fluffy tails.

8:

Finally I give him some ground shadow.

Simon Draws : A Tabby Cat

1:

I start like I'm drawing a normal cat with two big round eyes.

2:

Then the M-shaped ears...

3:

And a happy smile.

4:

I'm going to draw him standing up so you can see his pattern.

5:

I draw his front paws and his back like this with his belly underneath.

6:

There's his tail and rear legs.

7:

Tabby cats have a little M-shape above the eyes. This is a classic tabby so he has a large swirly pattern on the side.

8:

Finally all tabby cats have striped legs and a striped tail.

Simon Draws : A Squirrel

1:

I start with two large eyes and a little U-shaped nose.

2:

They have tiny little round ears.

3:

And they have big pouchy fluffy cheeks.

4:

Their bodies are quite bottle-shaped. I draw a line for the back.

5:

I give squirrels little arms.

6:

And I add little hands.

7:

Now here are his little rodent feet. These are similar to how I draw feet on hedgehogs.

8:

And of course what makes a squirrel is his great big fluffy tail.

Acknowledgments

Thanks to: Zöe Herbert-Jackson, Chris Gavin, Mike Cook, Elena Turtas, Jon Dunleavy, Filipe Alcada, Tom Bristow, Olly Wilks, Nigel Pay, Daniel Greaves, Mike Bell. Robert Kirby and Duncan Hayes at UA. Nick Davies and the Canongate team. Johnny Temple and the Akashic team. Everyone at Stray Cay Rescue and my cats Maisy, Jess, Hugh, and Teddy.

Simon Tofield is an award-winning animator and cartoonist who has always expressed himself through drawing. He has had a lifelong interest in animals, beginning as a child, when his uncle gave him a plastic pond which quickly filled with wildlife. Simon was given his first cat when he was nine and now has four rescue cats which are the mischievous inspiration for his work.

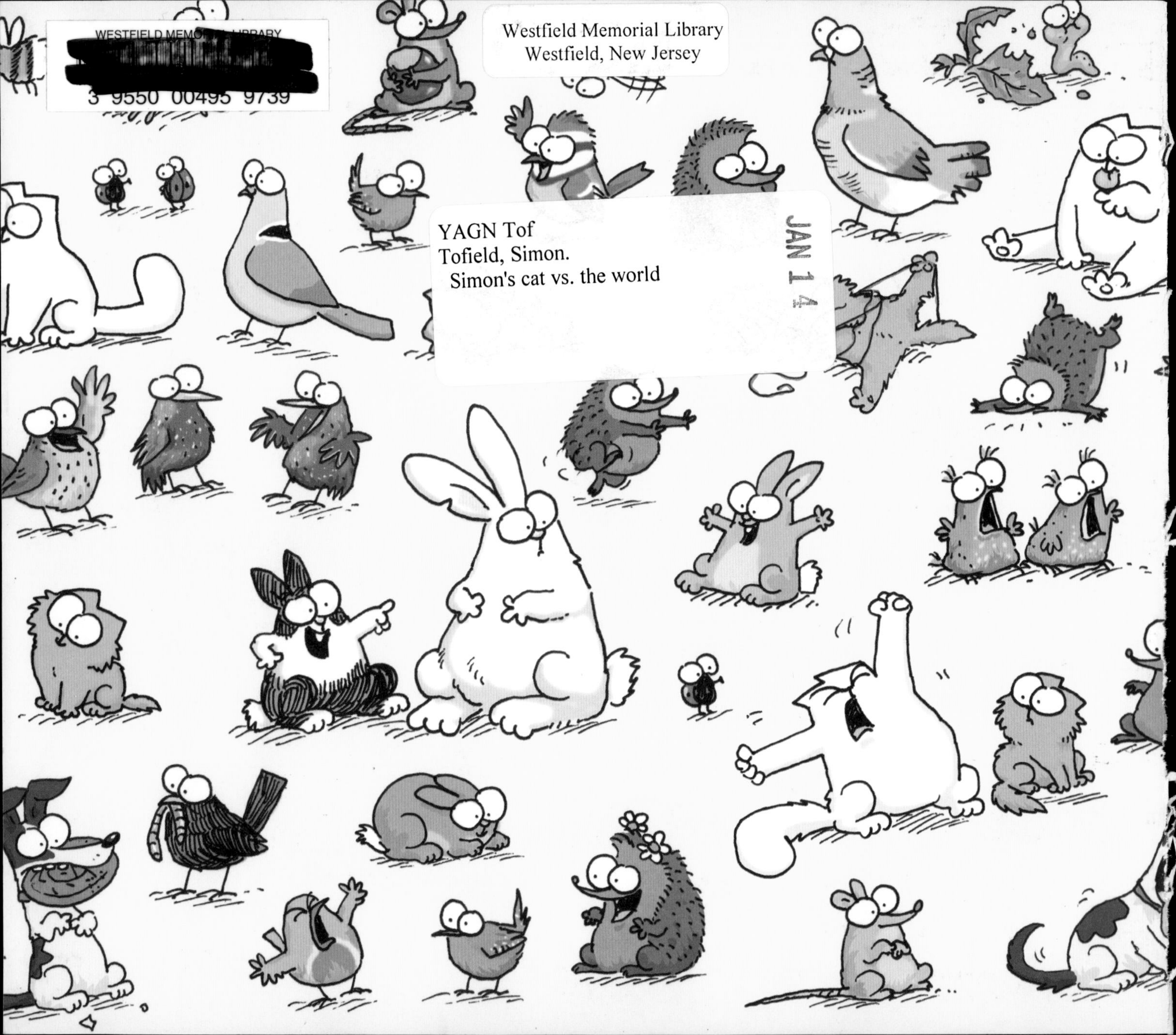